D1492121

ROBERT GRAVES

Poems Selected by Himself

WITHDRAWN

PENGUIN BOOKS

Penguin Books Ltd, Harmondsworth, Middlesex, England
Penguin Books Australia Ltd, Ringwood, Victoria, Australia

—

Published in Penguin Books 1957
Revised and enlarged edition 1961
Third edition 1966
Reprinted 1968
Fourth edition 1972

—

Copyright © Robert Graves, 1961, 1966, 1972

—

Made and printed in Great Britain
by Richard Clay (The Chaucer Press), Ltd,
Bungay, Suffolk
Set in Monotype Bembo

Foreword

Messrs Cassell kindly allow me to make this new, revised selection from their volumes, where the remainder of my work appears:

Collected Poems, 1959
More Poems, 1961
New Poems, 1962
Man Does, Woman Is, 1964
Love Respelt, 1965
Poems 1965–68

R. G.

Deyá, Majorca, Spain

Contents

THE HAUNTED HOUSE	15
REPROACH	16
THE FINDING OF LOVE	16
ROCKY ACRES	17
OUTLAWS	18
ONE HARD LOOK	20
A FROSTY NIGHT	20
ALLIE	21
LOVE WITHOUT HOPE	23
WHAT DID I DREAM?	23
THE TROLL'S NOSEGAY	23
THE HILLS OF MAY	24
LOST LOVE	25
VAIN AND CARELESS	26
THE PIER-GLASS	27
ANGRY SAMSON	28
APPLES AND WATER	29
DOWN	30
THIEF	31
IN PROCESSION	32
WARNING TO CHILDREN	34
THE COOL WEB	36
ALICE	36
THE BARDS	38
ANCESTORS	38
LOVE IN BARRENNESS	40
SONG OF CONTRARIETY	40
THE PRESENCE	41
THE LAND OF WHIPPERGINNY	42
IN NO DIRECTION	42
THE CASTLE	43
RETURN	44
NOBODY	45

FULL MOON   46
CONJUNCTION   47
VANITY   47
PURE DEATH   48
IT WAS ALL VERY TIDY   49
THESEUS AND ARIADNE   50
THE FURIOUS VOYAGE   51
SONG: LIFT BOY   52
ULYSSES   52
THE READER OVER MY SHOULDER   53
THE LEGS   54
FLYING CROOKED   56
GARDENER   56
FRAGMENT OF A LOST POEM   57
IN BROKEN IMAGES   57
ON RISING EARLY   58
THE DEVIL'S ADVICE TO STORY-TELLERS   58
SEA SIDE   59
WM. BRAZIER   60
WELSH INCIDENT   61
A FORMER ATTACHMENT   62
HELL   63
LOST ACRES   63
AT FIRST SIGHT   64
SYNTHETIC SUCH   65
DOWN, WANTON, DOWN!   65
ANY HONEST HOUSEWIFE   66
NATURE'S LINEAMENTS   66
TIME   67
THE PHILOSOPHER   68
ON DWELLING   69
OGRES AND PYGMIES   70
NEVER SUCH LOVE   71
TO WALK ON HILLS   72
ON PORTENTS   73
TO BRING THE DEAD TO LIFE   74
TO EVOKE POSTERITY   75

THE CUIRASSIERS OF THE FRONTIER 76
THE LAUREATE 77
LIKE SNOW 77
A JEALOUS MAN 78
THE CLOAK 79
THE FOREBODING 80
WITH HER LIPS ONLY 81
THE HALLS OF BEDLAM 82
A COUNTRY MANSION 83
ADVOCATES 86
THE TERRACED VALLEY 86
THE CHINK 87
THE AGES OF OATH 88
END OF PLAY 89
THE FALLEN TOWER OF SILOAM 90
THE GREAT-GRANDMOTHER 90
NO MORE GHOSTS 92
A LOVE STORY 93
DAWN BOMBARDMENT 94
THE SHOT 94
THE THIEVES 95
LOLLOCKS 95
TO SLEEP 97
DESPITE AND STILL 98
THE SUICIDE IN THE COPSE 98
FRIGHTENED MEN 99
LANGUAGE OF THE SEASONS 100
MID-WINTER WAKING 100
THE BEACH 101
THE VILLAGERS AND DEATH 101
THE DOOR 102
UNDER THE POT 102
THROUGH NIGHTMARE 103
SHE TELLS HER LOVE WHILE HALF ASLEEP 103
TO JUAN AT THE WINTER SOLSTICE 104
THE DEATH ROOM 105
TO BE CALLED A BEAR 106

MY NAME AND I 106
THE PERSIAN VERSION 108
1805 108
CONVERSATION PIECE 109
GROTESQUES I, II, III, IV, V, VI 110
THE SURVIVOR 112
BEAUTY IN TROUBLE 113
SIROCCO AT DEYÁ 114
YOUR PRIVATE WAY 115
THE WHITE GODDESS 115
THE SONG OF BLODEUWEDD 116
INSTRUCTIONS TO THE ORPHIC ADEPT 117
LAMENT FOR PASIPHAË 119
COUNTING THE BEATS 119
QUESTIONS IN A WOOD 120
DARIEN 121
THE PORTRAIT 123
PROMETHEUS 124
THE STRAW 124
DIALOGUE ON THE HEADLAND 125
A LOST JEWEL 126
THE SEA HORSE 127
CAT-GODDESSES 127
THE BLUE-FLY 128
THE WINDOW SILL 128
SPOILS 129
RHEA 130
GRATITUDE FOR A NIGHTMARE 131
THE NAKED AND THE NUDE 131
A SLICE OF WEDDING CAKE 132
CALL IT A GOOD MARRIAGE 133
AROUND THE MOUNTAIN 134
THE FACE IN THE MIRROR 135
SYMPTOMS OF LOVE 136
THE VISITATION 136
TROUGHS OF SEA 137
THE STARRED COVERLET 138

TURN OF THE MOON   138
SELDOM YET NOW   139
APPLE ISLAND   140
HORIZON   140
I'D DIE FOR YOU   141
THE WREATH   141
LION LOVER   142
IN HER PRAISE   142
A RESTLESS GHOST   143
BEWARE, MADAM!   143
HEDGES FREAKED WITH SNOW   144
IN TIME   145
SHE IS NO LIAR   145
A LAST POEM   145
TO BEGUILE AND BETRAY   146
I WILL WRITE   146
BIRD OF PARADISE   147
SONG: SWORD AND ROSE   147
ABOVE THE EDGE OF DOOM   148
THE GREEN CASTLE   148
NOT TO SLEEP   149
WHOLE LOVE   150
THE IMPOSSIBLE   150
IRON PALACE   151
EVERYWHERE IS HERE   152
SONG: THE FAR SIDE OF YOUR MOON   152
LEAVING THE REST UNSAID   153
DEAD HAND   154
LURE OF MURDER   154
ARREARS OF MOONLIGHT   155
WHAT DID YOU SAY?   155
ALL EXCEPT HANNIBAL   155
STOLEN JEWEL   156
THE SNAPPED THREAD   156
ECSTASY OF CHAOS   157
DANCING FLAME   157
BIRTH OF ANGELS   158

FORTUNATE CHILD   158
LOVING TRUE, FLYING BLIND   158
THE NEAR ECLIPSE   159
LIKE OWLS   159
ON GIVING   160
IN PERSPECTIVE   160
THE P'ENG THAT WAS A K'UN   161
BOWER-BIRD   161
THE UTTER RIM   162
UNICORN AND THE WHITE DOE   162
A DREAM OF HELL   164
OUR SELF   165
PERFECTIONISTS   165
THE NECKLACE   165
BITES AND KISSES   166
SPITE OF MIRRORS   167
A BRACELET   168
HOODED FLAME   168
THE CRANE   168
HER BRIEF WITHDRAWAL   169
STRANGENESS   169
SONG: THOUGH ONCE TRUE LOVERS   170
SONG: THE PALM TREE   170
SONG: DEWDROP AND DIAMOND   171
SONG: JUST FRIENDS   171
SONG: SULLEN MOODS   172
POSSIBLY   173
IS NOW THE TIME?   173
TWINS   174
SAIL AND OAR   174
GOOSEFLESH ABBEY   174
WIGS AND BEARDS   174
ASTYMELUSA   175
TO BE IN LOVE   176
FACT OF THE ACT   176
WITHIN REASON   177
SHE TO HIM   178

THE YET UNSAYABLE   178
THE OLIVE-YARD   179
THE NARROW SEA   179

Index of First Lines   180

The Haunted House

'Come, surly fellow, come: a song!'
  What, fools? Sing to you?
Choose from the clouded tales of wrong
  And terror I bring to you:

Of a night so torn with cries,
  Honest men sleeping
Start awake with rabid eyes,
  Bone-chilled, flesh creeping,

Of spirits in the web-hung room
  Up above the stable,
Groans, knockings in the gloom,
  The dancing table,

Of demons in the dry well
  That cheep and mutter,
Clanging of an unseen bell,
  Blood choking the gutter,

Of lust frightful, past belief,
  Lurking unforgotten,
Unrestrainable endless grief
  In breasts long rotten.

A song? What laughter or what song
  Can this house remember?
Do flowers and butterflies belong
  To a blind December?

Reproach

Your grieving moonlight face looks down
  Through the forest of my fears,
Crowned with a spiny bramble-crown,
  Bedewed with evening tears.

Why do you say 'untrue, unkind',
  Reproachful eyes that vex my sleep?
Straining in memory, I can find
  No cause why you should weep.

Untrue? But when, what broken oath?
  Unkind? I know not even your name.
Unkind, untrue, you brand me both,
  Scalding my heart with shame.

The black trees shudder, dropping snow,
  The stars tumble and spin.
Speak, speak, or how may a child know
  His ancestral sin?

The Finding of Love

Pale at first and cold,
Like wizard's lily-bloom
Conjured from the gloom,
Like torch of glow-worm seen
Through grasses shining green
By children half in fright,
Or Christmas candlelight
Flung on the outer snow,
Or tinsel stars that show

Their evening glory
With sheen of fairy story –

Now with his blaze
Love dries the cobweb maze
Dew-sagged upon the corn,
He brings the flowering thorn,
Mayfly and butterfly,
And pigeons in the sky,
Robin and thrush,
And the long bulrush,
Bird-cherry under the leaf,
Earth in a silken dress,
With end to grief,
With joy in steadfastness.

Rocky Acres

This is a wild land, country of my choice,
With harsh craggy mountain, moor ample and bare.
Seldom in these acres is heard any voice
But voice of cold water that runs here and there
Through rocks and lank heather growing without care.
No mice in the heath run, no song-birds fly
For fear of the buzzard that floats in the sky.

He soars and he hovers, rocking on his wings,
He scans his wide parish with a sharp eye,
He catches the trembling of small things,
He tears them in pieces, dropping from the sky;
Tenderness and pity the heart will deny,
Where life is but nourished by water and rock –
A hardy adventure, full of fear and shock.

Time has never journeyed to this lost land,
Crakeberry and heather bloom out of date,
The rocks jut, the streams flow singing on either hand,
Careless if the season be early or late,
The skies wander overhead, now blue, now slate;
Winter could be known by his cutting snow
If June did not borrow his armour also.

Yet this is my country, beloved by me best,
The first land that rose from Chaos and the Flood,
Nursing no valleys for comfort and rest,
Trampled by no shod hooves, bought with no blood.
Sempiternal country whose barrows have stood
Stronghold for demigods when on earth they go,
Terror for fat burghers on far plains below.

Outlaws

Owls – they whinny down the night;
    Bats go zigzag by.
Ambushed in shadow beyond sight
    The outlaws lie.

Old gods, tamed to silence, there
    In the wet woods they lurk,
Greedy of human stuff to snare
    In nets of murk.

Look up, else your eye will drown
    In a moving sea of black;
Between the tree-tops, upside down,
    Goes the sky-track.

Look up, else your feet will stray
    Into that ambuscade
Where spider-like they trap their prey
    With webs of shade.

For though creeds whirl away in dust,
    Faith dies and men forget,
These agèd gods of power and lust
    Cling to life yet –

Old gods almost dead, malign,
    Starving for unpaid dues:
Incense and fire, salt, blood and wine
    And a drumming muse,

Banished to woods and a sickly moon,
    Shrunk to mere bogey things,
Who spoke with thunder once at noon
    To prostrate kings:

With thunder from an open sky
    To warrior, virgin, priest,
Bowing in fear with a dazzled eye
    Towards the dread East –

Proud gods, humbled, sunk so low,
    Living with ghosts and ghouls,
And ghosts of ghosts and last year's snow
    And dead toadstools.

One Hard Look

Small gnats that fly
In hot July
And lodge in sleeping ears
Can rouse therein
A trumpet's din
With Day of Judgement fears.

Small mice at night
Can wake more fright
Than lions at midday;
A straw will crack
The camel's back –
There is no easier way.

One smile relieves
A heart that grieves
Though deadly sad it be,
And one hard look
Can close the book
That lovers love to see.

A Frosty Night

'Alice, dear, what ails you,
    Dazed and lost and shaken?
Has the chill night numbed you?
    Is it fright you have taken?'

'Mother, I am very well,
    I was never better.
Mother, do not hold me so,
    Let me write my letter.'

'Sweet, my dear, what ails you?'
    'No, but I am well.
The night was cold and frosty –
    There's no more to tell.'

'Ay, the night was frosty,
    Coldly gaped the moon,
Yet the birds seemed twittering
    Through green boughs of June.

'Soft and thick the snow lay,
    Stars danced in the sky –
Not all the lambs of May-day
    Skip so bold and high.

'Your feet were dancing, Alice,
    Seemed to dance on air,
You looked a ghost or angel
    In the star-light there.

'Your eyes were frosted star-light;
    Your heart, fire and snow.
Who was it said, "I love you"?'
    'Mother, let me go!'

Allie

Allie, call the birds in,
    The birds from the sky!
Allie calls, Allie sings,
    Down they all fly:

First there came
Two white doves,
  Then a sparrow from his nest,
Then a clucking bantam hen,
  Then a robin red-breast.

Allie, call the beasts in,
  The beasts, every one!
Allie calls, Allie sings,
  In they all run:
First there came
Two black lambs,
  Then a grunting Berkshire sow,
Then a dog without a tail,
  Then a red and white cow.

Allie, call the fish up,
  The fish from the stream!
Allie calls, Allie sings,
  Up they all swim:
First there came
Two goldfish,
  A minnow and a miller's thumb,
Then a school of little trout,
  Then the twisting eels come.

Allie, call the children,
  Call them from the green!
Allie calls, Allie sings,
  Soon they run in:
First there came
Tom and Madge,
  Kate and I who'll not forget
How we played by the water's edge
  Till the April sun set.

Love without Hope

Love without hope, as when the young bird-catcher
Swept off his tall hat to the Squire's own daughter,
So let the imprisoned larks escape and fly
Singing about her head, as she rode by.

What did I Dream?

What did I dream? I do not know –
    The fragments fly like chaff.
Yet, strange, my mind was tickled so
    I cannot help but laugh.

Pull the curtains close again,
    Tuck me grandly in;
Must a world of humour wane
    Because birds begin

Complaining in a fretful tone,
    Rousing me from sleep –
The finest entertainment known,
    And given rag-cheap?

The Troll's Nosegay

A simple nosegay! was that much to ask?
(Winter still nagged, with scarce a bud yet showing.)
He loved her ill, if he resigned the task.
'Somewhere,' she cried, 'there must be blossom blowing.'

It seems my lady wept and the troll swore
By Heaven he hated tears: he'd cure her spleen –
Where she had begged one flower he'd shower fourscore,
A bunch fit to amaze a China Queen.

Cold fog–drawn Lily, pale mist-magic Rose
He conjured, and in a glassy cauldron set
With elfin unsubstantial Mignonette
And such vague bloom as wandering dreams enclose.
But she?
      Awed,
            Charmed to tears,
                      Distracted,
                              Yet –
Even yet, perhaps, a trifle piqued – who knows?

The Hills of May

Walking with a virgin heart.
   The green hills of May,
Me, the Wind, she took as lover
   By her side to play,

Let me toss her untied hair,
   Let me shake her gown,
Careless though the daisies redden,
   Though the sun frown,

Scorning in her gay habit
   Lesser love than this,
My cool spiritual embracing,
   My secret kiss.

So she walked, the proud lady,
  So she danced or ran,
So she loved with a whole heart,
  Neglecting man. . . .

Fade, fail, innocent stars
  On the green of May:
She has left our bournes for ever,
  Too fine to stay.

Lost Love

His eyes are quickened so with grief,
He can watch a grass or leaf
Every instant grow; he can
Clearly through a flint wall see,
Or watch the startled spirit flee
From the throat of a dead man.
  Across two counties he can hear
And catch your words before you speak.
The woodlouse or the maggot's weak
Clamour rings in his sad ear,
And noise so slight it would surpass
Credence – drinking sound of grass,
Worm talk, clashing jaws of moth
Chumbling holes in cloth;
The groan of ants who undertake
Gigantic loads for honour's sake
(Their sinews creak, their breath comes thin);
Whir of spiders when they spin,
And minute whispering, mumbling, sighs
Of idle grubs and flies.
  This man is quickened so with grief,

He wanders god-like or like thief
Inside and out, below, above,
Without relief seeking lost love.

Vain and Careless

Lady, lovely lady,
    Careless and gay!
Once, when a beggar called,
    She gave her child away.

The beggar took the baby,
    Wrapped it in a shawl –
'Bring him back,' the lady said,
    'Next time you call.'

Hard by lived a vain man,
    So vain and so proud
He would walk on stilts
    To be seen by the crowd,

Up above the chimney pots,
    Tall as a mast –
And all the people ran about
    Shouting till he passed.

'A splendid match surely,'
    Neighbours saw it plain,
'Although she is so careless,
    Although he is so vain.'

But the lady played bobcherry,
    Did not see or care,
As the vain man went by her,
    Aloft in the air.

This gentle-born couple
  Lived and died apart –
Water will not mix with oil,
  Nor vain with careless heart.

The Pier-Glass

Lost manor where I walk continually
A ghost, though yet in woman's flesh and blood.
Up your broad stairs mounting with outspread
    fingers
And sliding steadfast down your corridors
I come by nightly custom to this room,
And even on sultry afternoons I come
Drawn by a thread of time-sunk memory.

Empty, unless for a huge bed of state
Shrouded with rusty curtains drooped awry
(A puppet theatre where malignant fancy
Peoples the wings with fear). At my right hand
A ravelled bell-pull hangs in readiness
To summon me from attic glooms above
Service of elder ghosts; here, at my left,
A sullen pier-glass, cracked from side to side,
Scorns to present the face (as do new mirrors)
With a lying flush, but shows it melancholy
And pale, as faces grow that look in mirrors.

Is there no life, nothing but the thin shadow
And blank foreboding, never a wainscot rat
Rasping a crust? Or at the window-pane
No fly, no bluebottle, no starveling spider?
The windows frame a prospect of cold skies

Half-merged with sea, as at the first Creation –
Abstract, confusing welter. Face about,
Peer rather in the glass once more, take note
Of self, the grey lips and long hair dishevelled,
Sleep-staring eyes. Ah, mirror, for Christ's love
Give me one token that there still abides
Remote – beyond this island mystery,
So be it only this side Hope, somewhere,
In streams, on sun-warm mountain pasturage –
True life, natural breath; not this phantasma.

Angry Samson

Are they blind, the lords of Gaza
　　In their strong towers,
Who declare Samson pillow-smothered
　　And stripped of his powers?

O stolid Philistines,
　　Stare now in amaze
At my foxes running in your cornfields
　　With their tails ablaze,

At swung jaw-bone, at bees swarming
　　In the stark lion's hide,
At these, the gates of well-walled Gaza
　　A-clank to my stride.

Apples and Water

Dust in a cloud, blinding weather,
  Drums that rattle and roar!
A mother and daughter stood together
  By their cottage door.

'Mother, the heavens are bright like brass,
  The dust is shaken high,
With labouring breath the soldiers pass,
  Their lips are cracked and dry.

'Mother, I'll throw them apples down,
  I'll fetch them cups of water.'
The mother turned with an angry frown,
  Holding back her daughter.

'But, mother, see, they faint with thirst,
  They march away to war.'
'Ay, daughter, these are not the first
  And there will come yet more.

'There is no water can supply them
  In western streams that flow;
There is no fruit can satisfy them
  On orchard-trees that grow.

'Once in my youth I gave, poor fool
  A soldier apples and water;
And may I die before you cool
  Such drouth as his, my daughter.

Downstairs a clock had chimed, two o'clock only
Then outside from the hen-roost crowing came.
Why should the shift-wing call against the clock,
Three hours from dawn? Now shutters click and knock,
And he remembers a sad superstition
Unfitting for the sick-bed. . . . Turn aside,
Distract, divide, ponder the simple tales
That puzzled childhood; riddles, turn them over –
Half-riddles, answerless, the more intense.
Lost bars of music tinkling with no sense
Recur, drowning uneasy superstition.

Mouth open he was lying, this sick man,
And sinking all the while; how had he come
To sink? On better nights his dream went flying,
Dipping, sailing the pasture of his sleep,
But now (since clock and cock) had sunk him down
Through mattress, bed, floor, floors beneath, stairs, cellars,
Through deep foundations of the manse; still sinking
Through unturned earth. How had he magicked space
With inadvertent motion or word uttered
Of too-close-packed intelligence (such there are),
That he should penetrate with sliding ease
Dense earth, compound of ages, granite ribs
And groins? Consider: there was some word uttered,
Some abracadabra – then, like a stage-ghost,
Funereally with weeping, down, drowned, lost!

Oh, to be a child once more, sprawling at ease
On smooth turf of a ruined castle court.
Once he had dropped a stone between the slabs
That masked an ancient well, mysteriously

Plunging his mind down with it. Hear it go
Rattling and rocketing into secret void!
Count slowly: one, two, three! and echoes come
Fainter and fainter, merged in the general hum
Of bees and flies; only a thin draught rises
To chill the drowsy air. There he had lain
As if unborn, until life floated back
From the deep waters.
                    Oh, to renew now
That bliss of repossession, kindly sun
Forfeit for ever, and the towering sky.

Falling, falling! Day closed up behind him.
Now stunned by the violent subterrene flow
Of rivers whirling down to hiss below
On the flame-axis of this terrible earth;
Toppling upon their waterfall, O spirit. . . .

Thief

To the galleys, thief, and sweat your soul out
With strong tugging under the curled whips,
That there your thievishness may find full play.
Whereas, before, you stole rings, flowers and watches,
Oaths, jests and proverbs,
Yet paid for bed and board like an honest man,
This shall be entire thiefdom: you shall steal
Sleep from chain-galling, diet from sour crusts,
Comradeship from the damned, the ten-year-chained –
And, more than this, the excuse for life itself
From a craft steered toward battles not your own.

31

Often, half-way to sleep,
Not yet sunken deep –
The sudden moment on me comes
From a mountain shagged and steep,
With terrible roll of dream drums,
Reverberations, cymbals, horns replying,
When with standards flying,
Horsemen in clouds behind,
The coloured pomps unwind,
The Carnival wagons
With their saints and their dragons
On the scroll of my teeming mind:
The Creation and Flood
With our Saviour's Blood
And fat Silenus' flagons,
And every rare beast
From the South and East,
Both greatest and least,
On and on,
In endless, variant procession.
I stand at the top rungs
Of a ladder reared in the air,
And I rail in strange tongues,
So the crowds murmur and stare;
Then volleys again the blare
Of horns, and summer flowers
Fly scattering in showers,
And the sun leaps in the sky,
While the drums thumping by
Proclaim me. . . .
   Oh, then, when I wake,

Could I courage take
To renew my speech,
Could I stretch and reach
The flowers and the ripe fruit
Laid out at the ladder's foot,
Could I rip a silken shred
From the banner tossed ahead,
Could I call a double-flam
From the drums, could the goat
Horned with gold, could the ram
With a flank like a barn-door,
The dwarf, the blackamoor,
Could Jonah and the Whale
And the Holy Grail,
The Ape with his platter
Going clitter-clatter,
The Nymphs and the Satyr,
And every marvellous matter
Come before me here,
Standing near and clear –
Could I make it so that you
Might wonder at them too!
– Glories of land and sea,
Of Heaven glittering free,
Castles hugely built in Spain,
Glories of Cockaigne,
Of that spicy kingdom, Cand,
Of the Delectable Land,
Of the Land of Crooked Stiles,
Of the Fortunate Isles,
Of the more than three-score miles
That to Babylon lead
(A pretty city indeed
Built on a four-square plan),

Of the Land of the Gold Man
Whose eager horses whinny
In their cribs of gold,
Of the Land of Whipperginny,
Of the land where none grows old. . . .
But cowardly I tell,
Rather, of the Town of Hell –
A huddle of dirty woes
And houses in fading rows
Straggled through space:
Hell has no market-place,
Nor point where four ways meet,
Nor principal street,
Nor barracks, nor Town Hall,
Nor shops at all,
Nor rest for weary feet,
Nor theatre, square, or park,
Nor lights after dark,
Nor churches, nor inns,
Nor convenience for sins –
Neither ends nor begins,
Rambling, limitless, hated well,
This Town of Hell
Where between sleep and sleep I dwell.

Warning to Children

Children, if you dare to think
Of the greatness, rareness, muchness,
Fewness of this precious only
Endless world in which you say
You live, you think of things like this:

Blocks of slate enclosing dappled
Red and green, enclosing tawny
Yellow nets, enclosing white
And black acres of dominoes,
Where a neat brown paper parcel
Tempts you to untie the string.
In the parcel a small island,
On the island a large tree,
On the tree a husky fruit.
Strip the husk and pare the rind off:
In the kernel you will see
Blocks of slate enclosed by dappled
Red and green, enclosed by tawny
Yellow nets, enclosed by white
And black acres of dominoes,
Where the same brown paper parcel –
Children, leave the string alone!
For who dares undo the parcel
Finds himself at once inside it,
On the island, in the fruit,
Blocks of slate about his head,
Finds himself enclosed by dappled
Green and red, enclosed by yellow
Tawny nets, enclosed by black
And white acres of dominoes,
With the same brown paper parcel
Still unopened on his knee.
And, if he then should dare to think
Of the fewness, muchness, rareness,
Greatness of this endless only
Precious world in which he says
He lives – he then unties the string.

The Cool Web

Children are dumb to say how hot the day is,
How hot the scent is of the summer rose,
How dreadful the black wastes of evening sky,
How dreadful the tall soldiers drumming by.

But we have speech, to chill the angry day,
And speech, to dull the rose's cruel scent.
We spell away the overhanging night,
We spell away the soldiers and the fright.

There's a cool web of language winds us in,
Retreat from too much joy or too much fear:
We grow sea-green at last and coldly die
In brininess and volubility.

But if we let our tongues lose self-possession,
Throwing off language and its watery clasp
Before our death, instead of when death comes,
Facing the wide glare of the children's day,
Facing the rose, the dark sky and the drums,
We shall go mad no doubt and die that way.

Alice

When that prime heroine of our nation, Alice,
Climbing courageously in through the Palace
Of Looking-Glass, found it inhabited
By chessboard personages, white and red,
Involved in never-ending tournament,
She being of a speculative bent
Had long foreshadowed something of the kind,

Asking herself: 'Suppose I stood behind
And viewed the fireplace of Their drawing-room
From hearthrug level, why must I assume
That what I'd see would need to correspond
With what I now see? And the rooms beyond?'

Proved right, yet not content with what she had done,
Alice decided to increase her fun:
She set herself, with truly British pride
In being a pawn and playing for her side,
And simple faith in simple stratagem,
To learn the rules and moves and perfect them.
So prosperously there she settled down
That six moves only and she'd won her crown –
A triumph surely! But her greater feat
Was rounding these adventures off complete:
Accepting them, when safe returned again,
As queer but true, not only in the main
True, but as true as anything you'd swear to,
The usual three dimensions you are heir to.
For Alice though a child could understand
That neither did this chance-discovered land
Make nohow or contrariwise the clean
Dull round of mid-Victorian routine,
Nor did Victoria's golden rule extend
Beyond the glass: it came to the dead end
Where empty hearses turn about; thereafter
Began that lubberland of dream and laughter,
The red-and-white-flower-spangled hedge, the grass
Where Apuleius pastured his Gold Ass,
Where young Gargantua made whole holiday . . .
But further from our heroine not to stray,
Let us observe with what uncommon sense –
Though a secure and easy reference

Between Red Queen and Kitten could be found –
She made no false assumption on that ground
(A trap in which the scientist would fall)
That queens and kittens are identical.

The Bards

The bards falter in shame, their running verse
Stumbles, with marrow-bones the drunken diners
Pelt them for their delay.
It is a something fearful in the song
Plagues them – an unknown grief that like a churl
Goes commonplace in cowskin
And bursts unheralded, crowing and coughing,
An unpilled holly-club twirled in his hand,
Into their many-shielded, samite-curtained,
Jewel-bright hall where twelve kings sit at chess
Over the white-bronze pieces and the gold;
And by a gross enchantment
Flails down the rafters and leads off the queens –
The wild-swan-breasted, the rose-ruddy-cheeked
Raven-haired daughters of their admiration –
To stir his black pots and to bed on straw.

Ancestors

My New Year's drink is mulled to-night
    And hot sweet vapours roofward twine.
The shades cry *Gloria!* with delight
    As down they troop to taste old wine.

They crowd about the crackling fire,
    Impatient as the rites begin;
Mulled porto is their souls' desire –
    Porto well aged with nutmeg in.

'Ha,' cries the first, 'my Alma wine
    Of one-and-seventy years ago!'
The second cheers 'God bless the vine!'
    The third and fourth like cockerels crow:

They crow and clap their arms for wings,
    They have small pride or breeding left –
Two grey-beards, a tall youth who sings,
    A soldier with his cheek-bone cleft.

O *Gloria!* for each ghostly shape,
    That whiffled like a candle smoke,
Now fixed and ruddy with the grape
    And mirrored in the polished oak.

I watch their brightening boastful eyes,
    I hear the toast their glasses clink:
'May this young man in drink grown wise
    Die, as we also died, in drink!'

Their reedy voices I abhor,
    I am alive at least, and young.
I dash their swill upon the floor:
    Let them lap grovelling, tongue to tongue.

Love in Barrenness

Below the ridge a raven flew
And we heard the lost curlew
Mourning out of sight below.
Mountain tops were touched with snow;
Even the long dividing plain
Showed no wealth of sheep or grain,
But fields of boulders lay like corn
And raven's croak was shepherd's horn
Where slow cloud-shadow strayed across
A pasture of thin heath and moss.

The North Wind rose: I saw him press
With lusty force against your dress,
Moulding your body's inward grace
And streaming off from your set face;
So now no longer flesh and blood
But poised in marble flight you stood.
O wingless Victory, loved of men,
Who could withstand your beauty then?

Song of Contrariety

Far away is close at hand,
Close joined is far away,
Love shall come at your command
Yet will not stay.

At summons of your dream-despair
She might not disobey,
But slid close down beside you there,
And complaisant lay.

Yet now her flesh and blood consent
In the hours of day,
Joy and passion both are spent,
Twining clean away.

Is the person empty air,
Is the spectre clay,
That love, lent substance by despair,
Wanes and leaves you lonely there
On the bridal day?

The Presence

Why say 'death'? Death is neither harsh nor kind:
Other pleasures or pains could hold the mind
If she were dead. For dead is gone indeed,
Lost beyond recovery and need,
Discarded, ended, rotted underground –
Of whom no personal feature could be found
To stand out from the soft blur evenly spread
On memory, if she were truly dead.

But living still, barred from accustomed use
Of body and dress and motion, with profuse
Reproaches (since this anguish of her grew
Do I still love her as I swear I do?)
She fills the house and garden terribly
With her bewilderment, accusing me,
Till every stone and flower, table and book,
Cries out her name, pierces me with her look,
'You are deaf, listen!
You are blind, see!'
                    How deaf or blind,

When horror of the grave maddens the mind
With those same pangs that lately choked her breath,
Altered her substance, and made sport of death?

The Land of Whipperginny

Come closer yet, my honeysuckle, my sweetheart Jinny:
  A low sun is gilding the bloom of the wood –
Is it Heaven, or Hell, or the Land of Whipperginny
  That holds this fairy lustre, not yet understood?

For stern proud psalms from the chapel on the moors
  Waver in the night wind, their firm rhythm broken,
Lugubriously twisted to a howling of whores
  Or lent an airy glory too strange to be spoken.

Soon the risen Moon will peer down with pity,
  Drawing us in secret by an ivory gate
To the fruit-plats and fountains of her silver city
  Where lovers need not argue the tokens of fate.

In No Direction

To go in no direction
    Surely as carelessly,
Walking on the hills alone,
    I never found easy.

Either I sent leaf or stick
    Twirling in the air,
Whose fall might be prophetic,
    Pointing 'there',

Or in superstition
    Edged somewhat away
From a sure direction
    Yet could not stray,

Or undertook the climb
    That I had avoided
Directionless some other time,
    Or had not avoided,

Or called as companion
    An eyeless ghost
And held his no direction
    Till my feet were lost.

The Castle

Walls, mounds, enclosing corrugations
Of darkness, moonlight on dry grass.
Walking this courtyard, sleepless, in fever;
Planning to use – but by definition
There's no way out, no way out –
Rope-ladders, baulks of timber, pulleys,
A rocket whizzing over the walls and moat –
Machines easy to improvise.
                  No escape,
No such thing; to dream of new dimensions,
Cheating checkmate by painting the king's robe
So that he slides like a queen;
Or to cry, 'Nightmare, nightmare!'
Like a corpse in the cholera-pit
Under a load of corpses;
Or to run the head against these blind walls,

Enter the dungeon, torment the eyes
With apparitions chained two and two,
And go frantic with fear –
To die and wake up sweating by moonlight
In the same courtyard, sleepless as before.

Return

The seven years' curse is ended now
That drove me forth from this kind land,
Fom mulberry-bough and apple-bough
And gummy twigs the west wind shakes,
To drink the brine from crusted lakes
And grit my teeth on sand.

Now for your cold, malicious brain
And most uncharitable, cold heart,
You, too, shall clank the seven years' chain
On sterile ground for all time cursed
With famine's itch and flames of thirst,
The blank sky's counterpart.

The load that from my shoulder slips
Straightway upon your own is tied:
You, too, shall scorch your finger-tips
With scrabbling on the desert's face
Such thought I had of this green place,
Sent scapegoat for your pride.

Here, Robin on a tussock sits,
And Cuckoo with his call of hope
Cuckoos awhile, then off he flits,
While peals of dingle-dongle keep
Troop-discipline among the sheep
That graze across the slope.

A brook from fields of gentle sun
Through the glade its water heaves,
The falling cone would well-nigh stun
That Squirrel wantonly lets drop
When up he scampers to tree-top
And dives among the green.

But no, I ask a surer peace
Than vengeance on you could provide.
Then fear no ill from my release:
Be off, elude the curse, disgrace
Some other green and happy place –
This world of fools is wide.

Nobody

Nobody, ancient mischief, nobody,
Harasses always with an absent body.

Nobody coming up the road, nobody,
Like a tall man in a dark cloak, nobody.

Nobody about the house, nobody,
Like children creeping up the stairs, nobody.

Nobody anywhere in the garden, nobody,
Like a young girl quiet with needlework, nobody.

Nobody coming, nobody, not yet here,
Incessantly welcomed by the wakeful ear.

Until this nobody shall consent to die
Under his curse must everybody lie –

The curse of his envy, of his grief and fright,
Of sudden rape and murder screamed in the night.

Full Moon

As I walked out that sultry night,
  I heard the stroke of one.
The moon, attained to her full height,
  Stood beaming like the sun:
She exorcized the ghostly wheat
To mute assent in love's defeat,
  Whose tryst had now begun.

The fields lay sick beneath my tread,
  A tedious owlet cried,
A nightingale above my head
  With this or that replied –
Like man and wife who nightly keep
Inconsequent debate in sleep
  As they dream side by side.

Your phantom wore the moon's cold mask,
  My phantom wore the same;
Forgetful of the feverish task
  In hope of which they came,
Each image held the other's eyes
And watched a grey distraction rise
  To cloud the eager flame –

To cloud the eager flame of love,
  To fog the shining gate;
They held the tyrannous queen above
  Sole mover of their fate,
They glared as marble statues glare
Across the tessellated stair
  Or down the halls of state.

And now warm earth was Arctic sea,
   Each breath came dagger-keen;
Two bergs of glinting ice were we,
   The broad moon sailed between;
There swam the mermaids, tailed and finned,
And love went by upon the wind
   As though it had not been.

Conjunction

What happens afterwards, none need enquire:
They are poised there in conjunction, beyond time,
At an oak-tree top level with Paradise:
Its leafy tester unshaken where they stand
Palm to palm, mouth to mouth, beyond desire,
Perpetuating lark song, perfume, colour,
And the tremulous gasp of watchful winds,

Past all unbelief, we know them held
By peace and light and irrefragable love –
Twin paragons, our final selves, resistant
To the dull pull of earth dappled with shade:
Myself the forester, never known to abandon
His vigilant coursing of the greenwood's floor,
And you, dryad of dryads, never before
Yielding her whole heart to the enemy, man.

Vanity

Be assured, the Dragon is not dead
But once more from the pools of peace
Shall rear his fabulous green head.

47

The flowers of innocence shall cease
And like a harp the wind shall roar
And the clouds shake an angry fleece.

'Here, here is certitude,' you swore,
'Below this lightning-blasted tree.
Where once it struck, it strikes no more.

'Two lovers in one house agree.
The roof is tight, the walls unshaken.
As now, so must it always be.'

Such prophecies of joy awaken
The toad who dreams away the past
Under your hearth-stone, light-forsaken,

Who knows that certitude at last
Must melt away in vanity –
No gate is fast, no door is fast –

That thunder bursts from the blue sky,
That gardens of the mind fall waste,
That fountains of the heart run dry.

Pure Death

We looked, we loved, and therewith instantly
Death became terrible to you and me.
By love we disenthralled our natural terror
From every comfortable philosopher
Or tall, grey doctor of divinity:
Death stood at last in his true rank and order.

It happened soon, so wild of heart were we,
Exchange of gifts grew to a malady:

Their worth rose always higher on each side
Till there seemed nothing but ungivable pride
That yet remained ungiven, and this degree
Called a conclusion not to be denied.

Then we at last bethought ourselves, made shift
And simultaneously this final gift
Gave: each with shaking hands unlocks
The sinister, long, brass-bound coffin-box,
Unwraps pure death, with such bewilderment
As greeted our love's first acknowledgement.

It Was All Very Tidy

When I reached his place,
The grass was smooth,
The wind was delicate,
The wit well timed,
The limbs well formed,
The pictures straight on the wall:
It was all very tidy.

He was cancelling out
The last row of figures,
He had his beard tied up in ribbons,
There was no dust on his shoe,
Everyone nodded:
It was all very tidy.

Music was not playing,
There were no sudden noises,
The sun shone blandly,
The clock ticked:
It was all very tidy.

49

'Apart from and above all this,
I reassured myself,
'There is now myself.'
It was all very tidy.

Death did not address me,
He had nearly done:
It was all very tidy.

They asked, did I not think
It was all very tidy?

I could not bring myself
To laugh, or untie
His beard's neat ribbons,
Or jog his elbow,
Or whistle, or sing,
Or make disturbance.
I consented, frozenly,
He was unexceptionable:
It was all very tidy.

Theseus and Ariadne

High on his figured couch beyond the waves
He dreams, in dream recalling her set walk
Down paths of oyster-shell bordered with flowers,
Across the shadowy turf below the vines.
He sighs: 'Deep sunk in my erroneous past
She haunts the ruins and the ravaged lawns.'

Yet still unharmed it stands, the regal house
Crooked with age and overtopped by pines

Where first he wearied of her constancy,
And with a surer foot she goes than when
Dread of his hate was thunder in the air,
When the pines agonized with flaws of wind
And flowers glared up at her with frantic eyes.
Of him, now all is done, she never dreams
But calls a living blessing down upon
What he supposes rubble and rank grass;
Playing the queen to nobler company.

The Furious Voyage

So, overmasterful, to sea!
But hope no distant view of sail,
No growling ice, nor weed, nor whale,
Nor breakers perilous on the lee.

Though you enlarge your angry mind
Three leagues and more about the ship
And stamp till every puncheon skip,
The wake runs evenly behind.

And it has width enough for you,
This vessel, dead from truck to keel
With its unmanageable wheel,
A blank chart and a surly crew,

In ballast only due to fetch
The turning point of wretchedness
On an uncoasted, featureless
And barren ocean of blue stretch.

Song: Lift-Boy

Let me tell you the story of how I began:
I began as the boot-boy and ended as the boot-man,
With nothing in my pockets but a jack-knife and a button,
With nothing in my pockets but a jack-knife and a button,
With nothing in my pockets.

Let me tell you the story of how I went on:
I began as the lift-boy and ended as the lift-man,
With nothing in my pockets but a jack-knife and a button,
With nothing in my pockets but a jack-knife and a button,
With nothing in my pockets.

I found it very easy to whistle and play
With nothing in my head or my pockets all day,
With nothing in my pockets.

But along came Old Eagle, like Moses or David;
He stopped at the fourth floor and preached me Damnation:
'Not a soul shall be savèd, not one shall be savèd.
The whole First Creation shall forfeit salvation:
From knife-boy to lift-boy, from ragged to regal,
Not one shall be savèd, not you, not Old Eagle,
No soul on earth escapeth, even if all repent –'
So I cut the cords of the lift and down we went,
With nothing in our pockets.

Ulysses

To the much-tossed Ulysses, never done
    With woman whether gowned as wife or whore,
Penelope and Circe seemed as one:

She like a whore made his lewd fancies run,
    And wifely she a hero to him bore.

Their counter-changings terrified his way:
    They were the clashing rocks, Symplegades,
Scylla and Charybdis too were they;
Now angry storms frosting the sea with spray
    And now the lotus island's drunken ease.

They multiplied into the Sirens' throng,
    Forewarned by fear of whom he stood bound fast
Maddened and helpless, to the vessel's mast,
Yet would not stop his ears: daring their song
    He groaned and sweated till that shore was past.

One, two and many: flesh had made him blind,
    Flesh had one pleasure only in the act,
Flesh set one purpose only in the mind –
Triumph of flesh and afterwards to find
    Still those same terrors wherewith flesh was racked.

His wiles were witty and his fame far known,
Every king's daughter sought him for her own,
    Yet he was nothing to be won or lost.
    All lands to him were Ithaca: love-tossed
He loathed the fraud, yet would not bed alone.

The Reader over My Shoulder

You reading over my shoulder, peering beneath
My writing arm – I suddenly feel your breath
Hot on my hand or on my nape,
So interrupt my theme, scratching these few
Words on the margin for you, namely you,
Too-human shape fixed in that shape: –

All the saying of things against myself
And for myself I have well done myself.
What now, old enemy, shall you do
But quote and underline, thrusting yourself
Against me, as ambassador of myself,
In damned confusion of myself and you?

For you in strutting, you in sycophancy,
Have played too long this other self of me,
Doubling the part of judge and patron
With that of creaking grind-stone to my wit.
Know me, have done: I am a proud spirit
And you for ever clay. Have done!

The Legs

There was this road,
And it led up-hill,
And it led down-hill,
And round and in and out.

And the traffic was legs,
Legs from the knees down,
Coming and going,
Never pausing.

And the gutters gurgled
With the rain's overflow,
And the sticks on the pavement
Blindly tapped and tapped.

What drew the legs along
Was the never-stopping,
And the senseless, frightening
Fate of being legs.

Legs for the road,
The road for legs,
Resolutely nowhere
In both directions.

My legs at least
Were not in that rout:
On grass by the road-side
Entire I stood,

Watching the unstoppable
Legs go by
With never a stumble
Between step and step.

Though my smile was broad
The legs could not see,
Though my laugh was loud
The legs could not hear.

My head dizzied, then:
I wondered suddenly,
Might I too be a walker
From the knees down?

Gently I touched my shins.
The doubt unchained them:
They had run in twenty puddles
Before I regained them.

Flying Crooked

The butterfly, a cabbage-white,
(His honest idiocy of flight)
Will never now, it is too late,
Master the art of flying straight,
Yet has – who knows so well as I? –
A just sense of how not to fly:
He lurches here and here by guess
And God and hope and hopelessness.
Even the aerobatic swift
Has not his flying-crooked gift.

Gardener

Loveliest flowers, though crooked in their border,
And glorious fruit, dangling from ill-pruned boughs –
Be sure the gardener had not eye enough
To wheel a barrow between the broadest gates
Without a clumsy scraping.

Yet none could think it simple awkwardness;
And when he stammered of a garden-guardian,
That the smooth lawns came by angelic favour,
The pinks and pears in spite of his own blunders,
They nudged at this conceit.

Well, he had something, though he called it nothing –
An ass's wit, a hairy-belly shrewdness
That would appraise the intentions of his angel
By the very difference of his own confusion,
And bring the most to pass.

Fragment of a Lost Poem

O the clear moment, when from the mouth
A word flies, current immediately
Among friends; or when a loving gift astounds
As the identical wish nearest the heart;
Or when a stone, volleyed in sudden danger,
Strikes the rabid beast full on the snout!

Moments in never. . . .

In Broken Images

He is quick, thinking in clear images;
I am slow, thinking in broken images.

He becomes dull, trusting to his clear images;
I become sharp, mistrusting my broken images.

Trusting his images, he assumes their relevance;
Mistrusting my images, I question their relevance.

Assuming their relevance, he assumes the fact;
Questioning their relevance, I question the fact.

When the fact fails him, he questions his senses;
When the fact fails me, I approve my senses.

He continues quick and dull in his clear images;
I continue slow and sharp in my broken images –

He in a new confusion of his understanding;
I in a new understanding of my confusion.

On Rising Early

Rising early and walking in the garden
Before the sun has properly climbed the hill –
His rays warming the roof, not yet the grass
Which is white with dew still.

And not enough breeze to eddy a puff of smoke,
And out in the meadows a thick mist lying yet,
And nothing anywhere ill or noticeable –
Thanks indeed for that.

But was there ever a day with wit enough
To be always early, to draw the smoke up straight
Even at three o'clock of an afternoon,
To spare dullness or sweat?

Indeed, many such days I remember
That were dew-white and gracious to the last,
That ruled out meal-times, yet had no more hunger
Than was felt by rising a half-hour before breakfast,
Nor more fatigue – where was it that I went
So unencumbered, with my feet trampling
Like strangers on the past?

The Devil's Advice to Story-Tellers

Lest men suspect your tale to be untrue,
Keep probability – some say – in view.
But my advice to story-tellers is:
Weigh out no gross of probabilities,
Nor yet make diligent transcriptions of
Known instances of virtue, crime or love.

To forge a picture that will pass for true,
Do conscientiously what liars do –
Born liars, not the lesser sort that raid
The mouths of others for their stock-in-trade:
Assemble, first, all casual bits and scraps
That may shake down into a world perhaps;
People this world, by chance created so,
With random persons whom you do not know –
The teashop sort, or travellers in a train
Seen once, guessed idly at, not seen again;
Let the erratic course they steer surprise
Their own and your own and your readers' eyes;
Sigh then, or frown, but leave (as in despair)
Motive and end and moral in the air;
Nice contradiction between fact and fact
Will make the whole read human and exact.

Sea Side

Into a gentle wilderness and confusion,
Of here and there, of one and everyone,
Of windy sandhills by an unkempt sea,
Came two and two in search of symmetry,
Found symmetry of two in sea and sand,
In left foot, right foot, left hand and right hand.

The beast with two backs is a single beast,
Yet by his love of singleness increased
To two and two and two and two again,
Until, instead of sandhills, see, a plain
Patterned in two and two, by two and two –
And the sea parts in horror at a view
Of rows of houses coupling, back to back,

While love smokes from their common chimney-stack
With two-four-eight-sixteenish single same
Re-registration of the duple name.

Wm. Brazier

At the end of Tarriers' Lane, which was the street
We children thought the pleasantest in Town
Because of the old elms growing from the pavement
And the crookedness, when the other streets were straight,
[They were always at the lamp-post round the corner,
Those pugs and papillons and in-betweens,
Nosing and snuffling for the latest news]
Lived Wm. Brazier, with a gilded sign,
'Practical Chimney Sweep'. He had black hands,
Black face, black clothes, black brushes and white teeth;
He jingled round the town in a pony-trap,
And the pony's name was Soot, and Soot was black.
But the brass fittings on the trap, the shafts,
On Soot's black harness, on the black whip-butt,
Twinkled and shone like any guardsman's buttons.
Wasn't that pretty? And when we children jeered:
'Hellow, Wm. Brazier! Dirty-face Wm. Brazier!'
He would crack his whip at us and smile and bellow,
'Hello, my dears!' [If he were drunk, but otherwise:
'Scum off, you damned young milliners' bastards, you!']

Let them copy it out on a pink page of their albums,
Carefully leaving out the bracketed lines.
It's an old story – f's for s's –
But good enough for them, the suckers.

'But that was nothing to what things came out
From the sea-caves of Criccieth yonder.'
'What were they? Mermaids? dragons? ghosts?'
'Nothing at all of any things like that.'
'What where they, then?'

                     'All sorts of queer things,
Things never seen or heard or written about,
Very strange, un-Welsh, utterly peculiar
Things. Oh, solid enough they seemed to touch,
Had anyone dared it. Marvellous creation,
All various shapes and sizes, and no sizes,
All new, each perfectly unlike his neighbour,
Though all came moving slowly out together.'
'Describe just one of them.'

                          'I am unable.'
'What were their colours?'

                      'Mostly nameless colours,
Colours you'd like to see; but one was puce
Or perhaps more like crimson, but not purplish.
Some had no colour.'

                   'Tell me, had they legs?'
'Not a leg nor foot among them that I saw.'
'But did these things come out in any order?
What o'clock was it? What was the day of the week?
Who else was present? How was the weather?'
'I was coming to that. It was half-past three
On Easter Tuesday last. The sun was shining.
The Harlech Silver Band played *Marchog Jesu*
On thirty-seven shimmering instruments,
Collecting for Carnarvon's (Fever) Hospital Fund.
The populations of Pwllheli, Criccieth,

Portmadoc, Borth, Tremadoc, Penrhyndeudraeth,
Were all assembled. Criccieth's mayor addressed them
First in good Welsh and then in fluent English,
Twisting his fingers in his chain of office,
Welcoming the things. They came out on the sand,
Not keeping time to the band, moving seaward
Silently at a snail's pace. But at last
The most odd, indescribable thing of all,
Which hardly one man there could see for wonder
Did something recognizably a something.'
'Well, what?'
                        'It made a noise.'
                                    'A frightening noise?'
'No, no.'
            'A musical noise? A noise of scuffling?'
'No, but a very loud, respectable noise –
Like groaning to oneself on Sunday morning
In Chapel, close before the second psalm.'
'What did the mayor do?'
                            'I was coming to that.'

A Former Attachment

And glad to find, on again looking at it,
It meant even less to me than I had thought –
You know the ship is moving when you see
The boxes on the quayside slide away
And become smaller – and feel a calm delight
When the port's cleared and the coast out of sight,
And ships are few, each on its proper course,
With no occasion for approach or discourse.

Hell

Husks, rags and bones, waste-paper, excrement,
  Denied a soul whether for good or evil
And casually consigned to unfulfilment,
  Are pronged into his bag by the great-devil.

Or words repeated, over and over and over,
  Until their sense sickens and all but dies,
These the same devil like a ghoulish lover
  Will lay his hands upon and hypnotize.

From husks and rags and waste and excrement
  He forms the pavement-feet and the lift-faces;
He steers the sick words into Parliament
  To rule a dust-bin world with deep-sleep phrases.

When healthy words or people chance to dine
  Together in this rarely actual scene,
There is a love-taste in the bread and wine,
  Nor is it asked: 'Do you mean what you mean?'

But to their table-converse boldly comes
  The same great-devil with his brush and tray,
To conjure plump loaves from the scattered crumbs,
  And feed his false five thousands day by day.

Lost Acres

These acres, always again lost
    By every new ordnance-survey
And searched for at exhausting cost
    Of time and thought, are still away.

They have their paper-substitute –
   Intercalation of an inch
At the so-many-thousandth foot –
   And no one parish feels the pinch.

But lost they are, despite all care,
   And perhaps likeliest to be bound
Together in a piece somewhere,
   A plot of undiscovered ground.

Invisible, they have the spite
   To trick the tautest measuring-chain
And the exact theodolite
   Perched every side of them in vain.

Yet, be assured, we have no need
   To plot these acres of the mind
With prehistoric fern and reed
   And monsters such as heroes find.

Maybe they have their flowers, their birds,
   Their trees behind the phantom fence,
But of a substance without words:
   To walk there would be loss of sense.

At First Sight

'Love at first sight,' some say, misnaming
Discovery of twinned helplessness
Against the huge tug of procreation.

But friendship at first sight? This also
Catches fiercely at the surprised heart
So that the cheek blanches and then blushes.

Synthetic Such

'The sum of all the parts of Such –
   Of each laboratory scene –
Is Such.' While Science means this much
   And means no more, why, let it mean!

But were the science-men to find
   Some animating principle
Which gave synthetic Such a mind
   Vital, though metaphysical –

To Such, such an event, I think
   Would cause unscientific pain:
Science, appalled by thought, would shrink
   To its component parts again.

Down, Wanton, Down!

Down, wanton, down! Have you no shame
That at the whisper of Love's name,
Or Beauty's, presto! up you raise
Your angry head and stand at gaze?

Poor Bombard-captain, sworn to reach
The ravelin and effect a breach –
Indifferent what you storm or why,
So be that in the breach you die!

Love may be blind, but Love at last
Knows what is man and what mere beast;
Or Beauty wayward, but requires
More delicacy from her squires.

Tell me, my witless, whose one boast
Could be your staunchness at the post,
When were you made a man of parts
To think fine and profess the arts?

Will many-gifted Beauty come
Bowing to your bald rule of thumb,
Or Love swear loyalty to your crown?
Be gone, have done! Down, wanton, down!

Any Honest Housewife

Any honest housewife could sort them out,
Having a nose for fish, an eye for apples.
Is it any mystery who are the sound,
And who the rotten? Never, by her lights.

Any honest housewife who, by ill-fortune,
Ever engaged a slut to scrub for her
Could instantly distinguish from the workers
The lazy, the liars and the petty thieves.

Does this denote a sixth peculiar sense
Gifted to housewives for their vestal needs?
Or is it failure of the usual five
In all unthrifty writers on this head?

Nature's Lineaments

When mountain rocks and leafy trees
And clouds and things like these,
With edges,

Caricature the human face,
Such scribblings have no grace
Nor peace –

The bulbous nose, the sunken chin,
The ragged mouth in grin
Of cretin.

Nature is always so: you find
That all she has of mind
Is wind,

Retching among the empty spaces,
Ruffling the idiot grasses,
The sheeps' fleeces.

Whose pleasures are excreting, poking,
Havocking and sucking,
Sleepy licking.

Whose griefs are melancholy,
Whose flowers are oafish,
Whose waters, silly,
Whose birds, raffish,
Whose fish, fish.

Time

The vague sea thuds against the marble cliffs
And from their fragments age-long grinds
Pebbles like flowers.

Or the vague weather wanders in the fields,
And up spring flowers with coloured buds
Like marble pebbles.

The beauty of the flowers is Time, death-grieved;
The pebbles' beauty too is Time,
Life-wearied.

It is easy to admire a blowing flower
Or a smooth pebble flower-like freaked
By Time and vagueness.

Time is Time's lapse, the emulsive element coaxing
All obstinate locks and rusty hinges
To loving-kindness.

And am I proof against that lovesome pair,
Old age and childhood, twins in Time,
In sorrowful vagueness?

And will I not pretend the accustomed thanks:
Humouring age with filial flowers,
Childhood with pebbles?

The Philosopher

Three blank walls, a barred window with no view,
A ceiling within reach of the raised hands,
A floor blank as the walls.

And, ruling out distraction of the body –
Growth of the hair and nails, a prison diet,
Thoughts of escape –

Ruling out memory and fantasy,
The distant tramping of the gaoler's boots,
Visiting mice and such,

What solace here for a laborious mind!
What a redoubtable and single task
One might attempt here:

Threading a logic between wall and wall,
Ceiling and floor, more accurate by far
Than the cob-spider's.

Truth captured without increment of flies –
Spinning and knotting till the cell became
A spacious other head

In which the emancipated reason might
Learn in due time to walk at greater length
And more unanswerably.

On Dwelling

Courtesies of good-morning and good-evening
From rustic lips fail as the town encroaches:
Soon nothing passes but the cold quick stare
Of eyes that see ghosts, yet too many for fear.

Here I too walk, silent myself, in wonder
At a town not mine, though plainly coextensive
With mine, even in days coincident:
In mine I dwell, in theirs like them I haunt.

And the green country, should I turn again there?
My bumpkin neighbours loom even ghostlier:
Like trees they murmur or like blackbirds sing
Courtesies of good-morning and good-evening.

Those famous men of old, the Ogres –
They had long beards and stinking arm-pits,
They were wide-mouthed, long-yarded and great-
  bellied
Yet not of taller stature, Sirs, than you.
They lived on Ogre-Strand, which was no place
But the churl's terror of their vast extent,
Where every foot was three-and-thirty inches
And every penny bought a whole hog.
Now of their company none survive, not one,
The times being, thank God, unfavourable
To all but nightmare shadows of their fame;
Their images stand howling on the hill
(The winds enforced against those wide mouths),
Whose granite haunches country-folk salute
With May Day kisses, and whose knobbed knees.

So many feats they did to admiration:
With their enormous throats they sang louder
Than ten cathedral choirs, with their grand yards
Stormed the most rare and obstinate maidenheads,
With their strong-gutted and capacious bellies
Digested stones and glass like ostriches.
They dug great pits and heaped huge mounds,
Deflected rivers, wrestled with the bear
And hammered judgements for posterity –
For the sweet-cupid-lipped and tassel-yarded
Delicate-stomached dwellers
In Pygmy Alley, where with brooding on them
A foot is shrunk to seven inches
And twelve-pence will not buy a spare rib.

And who would judge between Ogres and Pygmies –
The thundering text, the snivelling commentary –
Reading between such covers he will marvel
How his own members bloat and shrink again.

Never such Love

Twined together and, as is customary,
For words of rapture groping, they
'Never such love,' swore, 'ever before was!'
Contrast with all loves that had failed or staled
Registered their own as love indeed.

And was this not to blab idly
The heart's fated inconstancy?
Better in love to seal the love-sure lips,
For truly love was before words were,
And no word given, no word broken.

When the name 'love' is uttered
(Love, the near-honourable malady
With which in greed and haste they
Each other do infect and curse)
Or, worse, is written down. . . .

Wise after the event, by love withered,
A 'never more!' most frantically
Sorrow and shame would proclaim
Such as, they'd swear, never before were:
True lovers even in this.

To Walk on Hills

To walk on hills is to employ legs
As porters of the head and heart
Jointly adventuring towards
Perhaps true equanimity.

To walk on hills is to see sights
And hear sounds unfamiliar.
When in wind the pine-tree roars,
When crags with bleatings echo,
When water foams below the fall,
Heart records that journey
As memorable indeed;
Head reserves opinion,
Confused by the wind.

A view of three shires and the sea!
Seldom so much at once appears
Of the coloured world, says heart.
Head is glum, says nothing.

Legs become weary, halting
To sprawl in a rock's shelter,
While the sun drowsily blinks
On head at last brought low –
This giddied passenger of legs
That has no word to utter.

Heart does double duty,
As heart, and as head,
With portentous trifling.
A castle, on its crag perched,
Across the miles between is viewed
With awe as across years.

Now a daisy pleases,
Pleases and astounds, even,
That on a garden lawn could blow
All summer long with no esteem.

And the buzzard's cruel poise,
And the plover's misery,
And the important beetle's
Blue-green-shiny back. . . .

To walk on hills is to employ legs
To march away and lose the day.
Confess, have you known shepherds?
And are they not a witless race,
Prone to quaint visions?
Not thus from solitude
(Solitude sobers only)
But from long hilltop striding.

On Portents

If strange things happen where she is,
So that men say that graves open
And the dead walk, or that futurity
Becomes a womb and the unborn are shed,
Such portents are not to be wondered at,
Being tourbillions in Time made
By the strong pulling of her bladed mind
Through that ever-reluctant element.

To Bring the Dead to Life

To bring the dead to life
Is no great magic.
Few are wholly dead:
Blow on a dead man's embers
And a live flame will start.

Let his forgotten griefs be now,
And now his withered hopes;
Subdue your pen to his handwriting
Until it prove as natural
To sign his name as yours.

Limp as he limped,
Swear by the oaths he swore;
If he wore black, affect the same;
If he had gouty fingers,
Be yours gouty too.

Assemble tokens intimate of him –
A watch, a cloak, a pen:
Around these elements then build
A home familiar to
The greedy revenant.

So grant him life, but reckon
That the grave which housed him
May not be empty now!
You in his spotted garments
Shall yourself lie wrapped.

To Evoke Posterity

To evoke posterity
Is to weep on your own grave,
Ventriloquizing for the unborn:
'Would you were present in flesh, hero!
What wreaths and junketings!'

And the punishment is fixed:
To be found fully ancestral,
To be cast in bronze for a city square,
To dribble green in times of rain
And stain the pedestal.

Spiders in the spread beard;
A life proverbial
On clergy lips a-cackle;
Eponymous institutes,
Their luckless architecture.

Two more dates of life and birth
For the hour of special study
From which all boys and girls of mettle
Twice a week play truant
And worn excuses try.

Alive, you have abhorred
The crowds on holiday
Jostling and whistling – yet would you air
Your death-mask, smoothly lidded,
Along the promenade?

The Cuirassiers of the Frontier

Goths, Vandals, Huns, Isaurian mountaineers,
Made Roman by our Roman sacrament,
We can know little (as we care little)
Of the Metropolis: her candled churches,
Her white-gowned pederastic senators,
The cut-throat factions of her Hippodrome,
The eunuchs of her draped saloons.

Here is the frontier, here our camp and place –
Beans for the pot, fodder for horses,
And Roman arms. Enough. He who among us
At full gallop, the bowstring to his ear,
Lets drive his heavy arrows, to sink
Stinging through Persian corslets damascened,
Then follows with the lance – he has our love.

The Christ bade Holy Peter sheathe his sword,
Being outnumbered by the Temple guard.
And this was prudence, the cause not yet lost
While Peter might persuade the crowd to rescue.
Peter renegued, breaking his sacrament.
With us the penalty is death by stoning,
Not to be made a bishop.

In Peter's Church there is no faith nor truth,
Nor justice anywhere in palace or court.
That we continue watchful on the rampart
Concerns no priest. A gaping silken dragon,
Puffed by the wind, suffices us for God.
We, not the City, are the Empire's soul:
A rotten tree lives only in its rind.

The Laureate

Like a lizard in the sun, though not scuttling
When men approach, this wretch, this thing of
    rage,
Scowls and sits rhyming in his horny age.

His time and truth he has not bridged to ours,
But shrivelled by long heliotropic idling
He croaks at us his out-of-date humours.

Once long ago here was a poet; who died.
See how remorse twitching his mouth proclaims
It was no natural death, but suicide.

Arrogant, lean, unvenerable, he
Still turns for comfort to the western flames
That glitter a cold span above the sea.

Like Snow

She, then, like snow in a dark night,
Fell secretly. And the world waked
With dazzling of the drowsy eye,
So that some muttered 'Too much light',
And drew the curtains close.
Like snow, warmer than fingers feared,
And to soil friendly;
Holding the histories of the night
In yet unmelted tracks.

A Jealous Man

To be homeless is a pride
To the jealous man prowling
Hungry down the night lanes,

Who has no steel at his side,
No drink hot in his mouth,
But a mind dream-enlarged,

Who witnesses warfare,
Man with woman, hugely
Raging from hedge to hedge:

The raw knotted oak-club
Clenched in the raw fist,
The ivy-noose well flung,

The thronged din of battle,
Gaspings of the throat-snared,
Snores of the battered dying,

Tall corpses, braced together,
Fallen in clammy furrows,
Male and female,

Or, among haulms of nettle
Humped, in noisome heaps,
Male and female.

He glowers in the choked roadway
Between twin churchyards,
Like a turnip ghost.

(Here, the rain-worn headstone,
There, the Celtic cross
In rank white marble.)

This jealous man is smitten,
His fear-jerked forehead
Sweats a fine musk;

A score of bats bewitched
By the ruttish odour
Swoop singing at his head;

Nuns bricked up alive
Within the neighbouring wall
Wail in cat-like longing.

Crow, cocks, crow loud,
Reprieve the doomed devil –
Has he not died enough?

Now, out of careless sleep,
She wakes and greets him coldly,
The woman at home,

She, with a private wonder
At shoes bemired and bloody –
His war was not hers.

The Cloak

Into exile with only a few shirts,
Some gold coin and the necessary papers.
But winds are contrary: the Channel packet
Time after time returns the sea-sick peer
To Sandwich, Deal or Rye. He does not land,
But keeps his cabin: so at last we find him
In humble lodgings maybe at Dieppe,
His shirts unpacked, his night-cap on a peg,
Passing the day at cards and swordsmanship

Or merry passages with chambermaids,
By night at his old work. And all is well –
The country wine wholesome although so sharp,
And French his second tongue; a faithful valet
Brushes his hat and brings him newspapers.
This nobleman is at home anywhere,
His castle being, the valet says, his title.
The cares of an estate would incommode
Such tasks as now his Lordship has in hand.
His Lordship, says the valet, contemplates
A profitable absence of some years.
Has he no friend at Court to intercede?
He wants none: exile's but another name
For an old habit of non-residence
In all but the recesses of his cloak.
It was this angered a great personage.

The Foreboding

Looking by chance in at the open window
    I saw my own self seated in his chair
With gaze abstracted, furrowed forehead,
    Unkempt hair.

I thought that I had suddenly come to die,
    That to a cold corpse this was my farewell,
Until the pen moved slowly upon paper
    And tears fell.

He had written a name, yours, in printed letters:
    One word on which bemusedly to pore –
No protest, no desire, your naked name,
    Nothing more.

Would it be tomorrow, would it be next year?
   But the vision was not false, this much I knew;
And I turned angrily from the open window
   Aghast at you.

Why never a warning, either by speech or look,
   That the love you cruelly gave me could not
      last?
Already it was too late: the bait swallowed,
   The hook fast.

With Her Lips Only

This honest wife, challenged at dusk
At the garden gate, under a moon perhaps,
In scent of honeysuckle, dared to deny
Love to an urgent lover: with her lips only,
Not with her heart. It was no assignation;
Taken aback, what could she say else?
For the children's sake, the lie was venial;
'For the children's sake', she argued with her
   conscience.

Yet a mortal lie must follow before dawn:
Challenged as usual in her own bed,
She protests love to an urgent husband,
Not with her heart but with her lips only;
'For the children's sake', she argues with her
   conscience,
'For the children' – turning suddenly cold
   towards them.

The Halls of Bedlam

Forewarned of madness:
In three days' time at dusk
The fit masters him.

How to endure those days?
(Forewarned is foremad)
'– Normally, normally.'

He will gossip with children,
Argue with elders,
Check the cash account.

'I shall go mad that day –'
The gossip, the argument,
The neat marginal entry.

His case is not uncommon,
The doctors pronounce;
But prescribe no cure.

To be mad is not easy,
Will earn him no more
Than a niche in the news.

Then to-morrow, children,
To-morrow or the next day
He resigns from the firm.

His boyhood's ambition
Was to become an artist –
Like any City man's.

To the walls and halls of Bedlam
The artist is welcome –
Bold brush and full palette.

Through the cell's grating
He will watch his children
To and from school.

'Suffer the little children
To come unto me
With their Florentine hair!'

A very special story
For their very special friends –
They burst in the telling:

Of an evil thing, armed,
Tap-tapping on the door,
Tap-tapping on the floor,
'On the third day at dusk.'

Father in his shirt-sleeves
Flourishing a hatchet –
Run, children, run!

No one could stop him,
No one understood;
And in the evening papers . . .

(Imminent genius,
Troubles at the office,
Normally, normally,
As if already mad.)

A Country Mansion

This ancient house so notable
For its gables and great staircase,
Its mulberry-trees and alleys of clipped yew,
Humbles the show of every near demesne.

At the beginning it acknowledged owners –
Father, son, grandson –
But then, surviving the last heirs of the line,
Became a place for life-tenancy only.

At the beginning, no hint of fate,
No rats and no hauntings;
In the garden, then, the fruit-trees grew
Slender and similar in long rows.

A bedroom with a low ceiling
Caused little fret at first;
But gradual generations of discomfort
Have bred an anger there to stifle sleep.

And the venerable dining-room,
Where port in Limerick glasses
Glows twice as red reflected
In the memory mirror of the waxed table –

For a time with paint and flowered paper
A mistress tamed its walls,
But pious antiquarian hands, groping,
Rediscovered the grey panels beneath.

Children love the old house tearfully,
And the parterres, how fertile!
Married couples under the testers hugging
Enjoy carnality's bliss as nowhere else.

A smell of mould from loft to cellar,
Yet sap still brisk in the oak
Of the great beams: if ever they use a saw
It will stain, as cutting a branch from a green tree.

. . . Old Parr had lived one hundred years and
   five
(So to King Charles he bragged)
When he did open penance, in a sheet,
For fornication with posterity.

Old Parr died; not so the mansion
Whose inhabitants, bewitched,
Pour their fresh blood through its historic veins
And, if a tile blow from the roof, tremble.

The last-born of this race of sacristans
Broke the long spell, departed;
They lay his knife and fork at every meal
And every evening warm his bed;

Yet cannot draw him back from the far roads
For trifling by the lily-pool
Or wine at the hushed table where they meet,
The guests of genealogy.

It was his childhood's pleasure-ground
And still may claim his corpse,
Yet foster-cradle or foster-grave
He will not count as home.

This rebel does not hate the house,
Nor its dusty joys impugn:
No place less reverend could provoke
So proud an absence from it.

He has that new malaise of time:
Gratitude choking with vexation
That he should opulently inherit
The goods and titles of the extinct.

Advocates

Fugitive firs and larches for a moment
Caught, past midnight, by our headlight beam
On that mad journey through unlasting lands
I cannot put a name to, years ago,
(And my companions drowsy-drunk) – those trees
Resume again their sharp appearance, perfect
Of spur and tassel, claiming memory,
Claiming affection: 'Will we be included
In the catalogue? Yes, yes?' they plead.

Green things, you are already there enrolled.
And should a new resentment gnaw in me
Against my dear companions of that journey
(Strangers already then, in thought and deed)
You shall be advocates, charged to deny
That all the good I lived with them is lost.

The Terraced Valley

In a deep thought of you and concentration
I came by hazard to a new region:
The unnecessary sun was not there,
The necessary earth lay without care –
For more than sunshine warmed the skin
Of the round world that was turned outside-in.

Calm sea beyond the terraced valley
Without horizon easily was spread,
As it were overhead,
Washing the mountain-spurs behind me:

The unnecessary sky was not there,
Therefore no heights, no deeps, no birds of the air.

Neat outside-inside, neat below-above,
Hermaphrodizing love.
Neat this-way-that-way and without mistake:
On the right hand could slide the left glove.
Neat over-under: the young snake
Through an unyielding shell his path could break.
Singing of kettles, like a singing brook,
Made out-of-doors a fireside nook.

But you, my love, where had you then your
    station?
Seeing that on this counter-earth together
We go not distant from each other;
I knew you near me in that strange region,
So searched for you, in hope to see you stand
On some near olive-terrace, in the heat,
The left-hand glove drawn on your right hand,
The empty snake's egg perfect at your feet –
But found you nowhere in the wide land,
And cried disconsolately, until you spoke
Immediate at my elbow, and your voice broke
This trick of time, changing the world about
To once more inside-in and outside-out.

The Chink

A sunbeam on the well-waxed oak,
    In shape resembling not at all
The ragged chink by which it broke
    Into this darkened hall,

Swims round and golden over me,
    The sun's plenipotentiary.

So may my round love a chink find:
    With such address to break
Into your grief-occluded mind
    As you shall not mistake
But, rising, open to me for truth's sake.

The Ages of Oath

To find a garden-tulip growing
Among wild primroses of a wild field,
Or a cuckoo's egg in a blackbird's nest,
Or a giant mushroom, a whole basketful –
The memorable feats of childhood!
Once, by the earthworks, scratching in the soil,
My stick turned up a Roman amber bead. . . .

The lost, the freakish, the unspelt
Drew me: for simple sights I had no eye.
And did I swear allegiance then
To wildness, not (as I thought) to truth –
Become a virtuoso, and this also,
Later, of simple sights, when tiring
Of unicorn and upas?

Did I forget how to greet plainly
The especial sight, how to know deeply
The pleasure shared by upright hearts?
And is this to begin afresh, with oaths
On the true book, in the true name,
Now stammering out my praise of you,
Like a boy owning his first love?

End of Play

We have reached the end of pastime, for always,
Ourselves and everyone, though few confess it
Or see the sky other than, as of old,
A foolish smiling Mary-mantle blue;

Though life may still seem to dawdle golden
In some June landscape among giant flowers,
The grass to shine as cruelly green as ever,
Faith to descend in a chariot from the sky –

May seem only: a mirror and an echo
Mediate henceforth with vision and sound.
The cry of faith, no longer mettlesome,
Sounds as a blind man's pitiful plea of 'blind'.

We have at last ceased idling, which to regret
Were as shallow as to ask our milk-teeth back;
As many forthwith do, and on their knees
Call lugubriously upon chaste Christ.

We tell no lies now, at last cannot be
The rogues we were – so evilly linked in sense
With what we scrutinized that lion or tiger
Could leap from every copse, strike and devour us.

No more shall love in hypocritic pomp
Conduct its innocents through a dance of shame,
From timid touching of gloved fingers
To frantic laceration of naked breasts.

Yet love survives, the word carved on a sill
Under antique dread of the headsman's axe;
It is the echoing mind, as in the mirror
We stare on our dazed trunks at the block kneeling.

The Fallen Tower of Siloam

Should the building totter, run for an archway!
We were there already – already the collapse
Powdered the air with chalk, and shrieking
Of old men crushed under the fallen beams
Dwindled to comic yelps. How unterrible
When the event outran the alarm
And suddenly we were free –

Free to forget how grim it stood,
That tower, and what wide fissures ran
Up the west wall, how rotten the under-pinning
At the south-eastern angle. Satire
Had whirled a gentle wind around it,
As if to buttress the worn masonry;
Yet we, waiting, had abstained from satire.

It behoved us, indeed, as poets
To be silent in Siloam, to foretell
No visible calamity. Though kings
Were crowned and gold coin minted still and horses
Still munched at nose-bags in the public streets,
All such sad emblems were to be condoned:
An old wives' tale, not ours.

The Great-Grandmother

That aged woman with the bass voice
And yellowing white hair: believe her.
Though to your grandfather, her son, she lied
And to your father disingenuously

Told half the tale as the whole,
Yet she was honest with herself,
Knew disclosure was not yet due,
Knows it is due now.

She will conceal nothing of consequence
From you, her great-grandchildren
(So distant the relationship,
So near her term),
Will tell you frankly, she has waited
Only for your sincere indifference
To exorcize that filial regard
Which has estranged her, seventy years,
From the folk of her house.

Confessions of old distaste
For music, sighs and roses –
Their false-innocence assaulting her,
Breaching her hard heart;
Of the pleasures of a full purse,
Of bright brass and clean linen,
Of being alone at last;
Disgust with the ailing poor
To whom she was bountiful;
How the prattle of young children
Vexed more than if they whined;
How she preferred cats.

She will say, yes, she acted well,
Took such pride in the art
That none of them suspected, even,
Her wrathful irony
In doing what they asked
Better than they could ask it . . .
But, ah, how grudgingly her will returned

After the severance of each navel-cord,
And fled how far again,
When again she was kind!

She has outlasted all man-uses,
As was her first resolve:
Happy and idle like a port
After the sea's recession,
She does not misconceive the nature
Of shipmen or of ships.
Hear her, therefore, as the latest voice;
The intervening generations (drifting
On tides of fancy still), ignore.

No More Ghosts

The patriarchal bed with four posts
Which was a harbourage of ghosts
Is hauled out from the attic glooms
And cut to wholesome furniture for wholesome rooms;

Where they (the ghosts) confused, abused, thinned,
Forgetful how they sighed and sinned,
Cannot disturb our ordered ease
Except as summer dust tickles the nose to sneeze.

We are restored to simple days, are free
From cramps of dark necessity,
And one another recognize
By an immediate love that signals at our eyes.

No new ghosts can appear. Their poor cause
Was that time freezes, and time thaws;
But here only such loves can last
As do not ride upon the weathers of the past.

A Love Story

The full moon easterly rising, furious,
Against a winter sky ragged with red;
The hedges high in snow, and owls raving –
Solemnities not easy to withstand:
A shiver wakes the spine.

In boyhood, having encountered the scene,
I suffered horror: I fetched the moon home,
With owls and snow, to nurse in my head
Throughout the trials of a new spring,
Famine unassuaged.

But fell in love, and made a lodgement
Of love on those chill ramparts.
Her image was my ensign: snows melted,
Hedges sprouted, the moon tenderly shone,
The owls trilled with tongues of nightingale.

These were all lies, though they matched the time,
And brought me less than luck: her image
Warped in the weather, turned beldamish.
Then back came winter on me at a bound,
The pallid sky heaved with a moon-quake.

Dangerous it has been with love-notes
To serenade Queen Famine.
In tears I recomposed the former scene,
Let the snow lie, watched the moon rise, suffered
    the owls,
Paid homage to them of unevent.

Dawn Bombardment

Guns from the sea open against us:
The smoke rocks bodily in the casemate
And a yell of doom goes up.
We count and bless each new, heavy concussion –
Captives awaiting rescue.

Visiting angel of the wild-fire hair
Who in dream reassured us nightly
Where we lay fettered,
Laugh at us, as we wake – our faces
So tense with hope the tears run down.

The Shot

The curious heart plays with its fears:
To hurl a shot through the ship's planks,
Being assured that the green angry flood
Is charmed and dares not dance into the hold –
Nor first to sweep a lingering glance around
For land or shoal or cask adrift.
'So miracles are done; but madmen drown.'

O weary luxury of hypothesis –
For human nature, honest human nature
(Which the fear-pampered heart denies)
Knows its own miracle: not to go mad.
Will pitch the shot in fancy, hint the fact,
Will bore perhaps a meagre auger hole
But stanch the spurting with a tarred rag,
And will not drown, nor even ride the cask.

The Thieves

Lovers in the act dispense
With such meum-tuum sense
As might warningly reveal
What they must not pick or steal,
And their nostrum is to say:
'I and you are both away.'

After, when they disentwine
You from me and yours from mine,
Neither can be certain who
Was that I whose mine was you.
To the act again they go
More completely not to know.

Theft is theft and raid is raid
Though reciprocally made.
Lovers, the conclusion is
Doubled sighs and jealousies
In a single heart that grieves
For lost honour among thieves.

Lollocks

By sloth on sorrow fathered,
These dusty-featured Lollocks
Have their nativity in all disordered
Backs of cupboard drawers.

They play hide and seek
Among collars and novels
And empty medicine bottles,

And letters from abroad
That never will be answered.

Every sultry night
They plague little children,
Gurgling from the cistern,
Humming from the air,
Skewing up the bed-clothes,
Twitching the blind.

When the imbecile agèd
Are over-long in dying
And the nurse drowses,
Lollocks come skipping
Up the tattered stairs
And are nasty together
In the bed's shadow.

The signs of their presence
Are boils on the neck,
Dreams of vexation suddenly recalled
In the middle of the morning,
Languor after food.

Men cannot see them,
Men cannot hear them,
Do not believe in them –
But suffer the more
Both in neck and belly.

Women can see them –
O those naughty wives
Who sit by the fireside
Munching bread and honey,
Watching them in mischief
From corners of their eyes,

Slily allowing them to lick
Honey-sticky fingers.

Sovereign against Lollocks
Are hard broom and soft broom,
To well comb the hair,
To well brush the shoe,
And to pay every debt
As it falls due.

To Sleep

The mind's eye sees as the heart mirrors:
Loving in part, I did not see you whole,
Grew flesh-enraged that I could not conjure
A whole you to attend my fever-fit
In a doubtful hour between a night and day
And be Sleep that had kept so long away.

Of you sometimes a hand, a brooch, a shoe
Wavered beside me, unarticulated –
As the vexed insomniac dream-forges;
And the words I chose for your voice to speak
Echoed my own voice with its dry creak.

Now that I love you, now that I recall
All scattered elements of will that swooped
By night as jealous dreams through windows
To circle above the beds like bats,
Or as dawn-birds flew blindly at the panes
In curiosity rattling out their brains –

Now that I love you, as not before,
Now you can be and say, as not before:
The mind clears and the heart true-mirrors you
Where at my side an early watch you keep
And all self-bruising heads loll into sleep.

Despite and Still

Have you not read
The words in my head,
And I made part
Of your own heart?
We have been such as draw
The losing straw –
You of your gentleness,
I of my rashness,
Both of despair –
Yet still might share
This happy will:
To love despite and still.
Never let us deny
The thing's necessity,
But, O, refuse
To choose
Where chance may seem to give
Loves in alternative.

The Suicide in the Copse

The suicide, far from content,
Stared down at his own shattered skull:
Was this what he meant?

Had not his purpose been
To liberate himself from duns and dolts
By a change of scene?

From somewhere came a roll of laughter:
He had looked so on his wedding-day,
And the day after.

There was nowhere at all to go,
And no diversion now but to peruse
What literature the winds might blow

Into the copse where his body lay:
A year-old sheet of sporting news,
A crumpled schoolboy essay.

Frightened Men

We were not ever of their feline race,
Never had hidden claws so sharp as theirs
In any half-remembered incarnation;
Have only the least knowledge of their minds
Through a grace on their part in thinking aloud;
And we remain mouse-quiet when they begin
Suddenly in their unpredictable way
To weave an allegory of their lives,
Making each point by walking round it –
Then off again, as interest is warmed.
What have they said? Or unsaid? What?
We understood the general drift only.

They are punctilious as implacable,
Most neighbourly to those who love them least.
A shout will scare them. When they spring, they seize.
The worst is when they hide from us and change

To something altogether other:
We meet them at the doors, as who returns
After a one-hour-seeming century
To a house not his own.

Language of the Seasons

Living among orchards, we are ruled
By the four seasons necessarily:
This from unseasonable frosts we learn
Or from usurping suns and haggard flowers –
Legitimist our disapproval.

Weather we knew, not seasons, in the city
Where, seasonless, orange and orchid shone,
Knew it by heavy overcoat or light,
Framed love in later terminologies
Than here, where we report how weight of snow,
Or weight of fruit, tears branches from the tree.

Mid-Winter Waking

Stirring suddenly from long hibernation,
I knew myself once more a poet
Guarded by timeless principalities
Against the worm of death, this hillside haunting;
And presently dared open both my eyes.

O gracious, lofty, shone against from under,
Back-of-the-mind-far-clouds like towers;
And you, sudden warm airs that blow
Before the expected season of new blossom,
While sheep still gnaw at roots and lambless go –

Be witness that on waking, this mid-winter,
I found her hand in mine laid closely
Who shall watch out the Spring with me.
We stared in silence all around us
But found no winter anywhere to see.

The Beach

Louder than gulls the little children scream
Whom fathers haul into the jovial foam;
But others fearlessly rush in, breast high,
Laughing the salty water from their mouths –
Heroes of the nursery.

The horny boatman, who has seen whales
And flying fishes, who has sailed as far
As Demerara and the Ivory Coast,
Will warn them, when they crowd to hear his tales,
That every ocean smells alike of tar.

The Villagers and Death

The Rector's pallid neighbour at The Firs,
Death, did not flurry the parishioners.
Yet from a weight of superstitious fears
Each tried to lengthen his own term of years.
He was congratulated who combined
Toughness of flesh and weakness of the mind
In consequential rosiness of face.
This dull and not ill-mannered populace
Pulled off their caps to Death, as they slouched by,
But rumoured him both atheist and spy.

All vowed to outlast him (though none ever did)
And hear the earth drum on his coffin-lid.
Their groans and whispers down the village street
Soon soured his nature, which was never sweet.

The Door

When she came suddenly in
It seemed the door could never close again,
Nor even did she close it – she, she –
The room lay open to a visiting sea
Which no door could restrain.

Yet when at last she smiled, tilting her head
To take her leave of me,
Where she had smiled, instead
There was a dark door closing endlessly,
The waves receded.

Under the Pot

Sulkily the sticks burn, and though they crackle
    With scorn under the bubbling pot, or spout
Magnanimous jets of flame against the smoke,
    At each heel end a dirty sap breaks out.

Confess, creatures, how sulkily ourselves
    We hiss with doom, fuel of a sodden age –
Not rapt up roaring to the chimney stack
    On incandescent clouds of spirit or rage.

Never be disenchanted of
That place you sometimes dream yourself into,
Lying at large remove beyond all dream,
Or those you find there, though but seldom
In their company seated –

The untameable, the live, the gentle.
Have you not known them? Whom? They carry
Time looped so river-wise about their house
There's no way in by history's road
To name or number them.

In your sleepy eyes I read the journey
Of which disjointedly you tell; which stirs
My loving admiration, that you should travel
Through nightmare to a lost and moated land,
Who are timorous by nature.

She Tells Her Love While Half Asleep

She tells her love while half asleep,
    In the dark hours,
        With half-words whispered low:
As Earth stirs in her winter sleep
    And puts out grass and flowers
        Despite the snow,
        Despite the falling snow.

To Juan at the Winter Solstice

There is one story and one story only
That will prove worth your telling,
Whether as learned bard or gifted child;
To it all lines or lesser gauds belong
That startle with their shining
Such common stories as they stray into.

Is it of trees you tell, their months and virtues,
Or strange beasts that beset you,
Of birds that croak at you the Triple will?
Or of the Zodiac and how slow it turns
Below the Boreal Crown,
Prison of all true kings that ever reigned?

Water to water, ark again to ark,
From woman back to woman:
So each new victim treads unfalteringly
The never altered circuit of his fate,
Bringing twelve peers as witness
Both to his starry rise and starry fall.

Or is it of the Virgin's silvery beauty,
All fish below the thighs?
She in her left hand bears a leafy quince;
When, with her right she crooks a finger, smiling,
How may the King hold back?
Royally then he barters life for love.

Or of the undying snake from chaos hatched,
Whose coils contain the ocean,
Into whose chops with naked sword he springs,

Then in black water, tangled by the reeds,
Battles three days and nights,
To be spewed up beside her scalloped shore?

Much snow is falling, winds roar hollowly,
The owl hoots from the elder,
Fear in your heart cries to the loving-cup:
Sorrow to sorrow as the sparks fly upward.
The log groans and confesses:
There is one story and one story only.

Dwell on her graciousness, dwell on her smiling,
Do not forget what flowers
The great boar trampled down in ivy time.
Her brow was creamy as the crested wave,
Her sea-blue eyes were wild
But nothing promised that is not performed.

The Death Room

Look forward, truant, to your second childhood.
The crystal sphere discloses
Wall-paper roses mazily repeated
In pink and bronze, their bunches harbouring
Elusive faces, under an inconclusive
Circling, spidery, ceiling craquelure,
And, by the window-frame, the well-loathed, lame,
Damp-patch, cross-patch, sleepless L-for-Lemur
Who, puffed to giant size,
Waits jealously till children close their eyes.

To be Called a Bear

Bears gash the forest trees
    To mark the bounds
    Of their own hunting grounds;
They follow the wild bees
    Point by point home
    For love of honeycomb;
They browse on blueberries.

Then should I stare
If I am called a bear,
And it is not the truth?
Unkempt and surly with a sweet tooth
I tilt my muzzle toward the starry hub
Where Queen Callisto guards her cub;

But envy those that here
    All winter breathing slow
    Sleep warm under the snow,
That yawn awake when the skies clear,
    And lank with longing grow
No more than one brief month a year.

My Name and I

The impartial Law enrolled a name
    For my especial use:
My rights in it would rest the same
Whether I puffed it into fame
    Or sank it in abuse.

Robert was what my parents guessed
   When first they peered at me,
And *Graves* an honourable bequest
With Georgian silver and the rest
   From my male ancestry.

They taught me: 'You are *Robert Graves*
   (Which you must learn to spell),
But see that *Robert Graves* behaves,
Whether with honest men or knaves,
   Exemplarily well.'

Then though my I was always I,
   Illegal and unknown,
With nothing to arrest it by –
As will be obvious when I die
   And *Robert Graves* lives on –

I cannot well repudiate
   This noun, this natal star,
This gentlemanly self, this mate
So kindly forced on me by fate,
   Time and the registrar;

And therefore hurry him ahead
   As an ambassador
To fetch me home my beer and bread
Or commandeer the best green bed,
   As he has done before.

Yet, understand, I am not he
   Either in mind or limb;
My name will take less thought for me,
In worlds of men I cannot see,
   Than ever I for him.

Truth-loving Persians do not dwell upon
The trivial skirmish fought near Marathon.
As for the Greek theatrical tradition
Which represents that summer's expedition
Not as a mere reconnaissance in force
By three brigades of foot and one of horse
(Their left flank covered by some obsolete
Light craft detached from the main Persian fleet)
But as a grandiose, ill-starred attempt
To conquer Greece – they treat it with contempt;
And only incidentally refute
Major Greek claims, by stressing what repute
The Persian monarch and the Persian nation
Won by this salutary demonstration:
Despite a strong defence and adverse weather
All arms combined magnificently together.

1805

At Viscount Nelson's lavish funeral,
    While the mob milled and yelled about St Paul's,
A General chatted with an Admiral:

'One of your Colleagues, Sir, remarked today
    That Nelson's *exit*, though to be lamented,
Falls not inopportunely, in its way.'

'He was a thorn in our flesh,' came the reply –
    'The most bird-witted, unaccountable,
Odd little runt that ever I did spy.

'One arm, one peeper, vain as Pretty Poll,
  A meddler, too, in foreign politics
And gave his heart in pawn to a plain moll.

'He would dare lecture us Sea Lords, and then
  Would treat his ratings as though men of honour
And play at leap-frog with his midshipmen!

'We tried to box him down, but up he popped,
  And when he'd banged Napoleon at the Nile
Became too much the hero to be dropped.

'You've heard that Copenhagen "blind" eye story?
  We'd tied him to Nurse Parker's apron-strings –
By G—d, he snipped them through and snatched the
    glory!'

'Yet,' cried the General, 'six-and-twenty sail
  Captured or sunk by him off Tráfalgár –
That writes a handsome *finis* to the tale.'

'Handsome enough. The seas are England's now.
  That fellow's foibles need no longer plague us.
He died most creditably, I'll allow.'

'And, Sir, the secret of his victories?'
  'By his unServicelike, familiar ways, Sir,
He made the whole Fleet love him, damn his eyes!'

Conversation Piece

  By moonlight
  At midnight,
  Under the vines,
  A hotel chair
  Settles down moodily before the headlines
  Of a still-folded evening newspaper.

The other chair
Of the pair
Lies on its back,
Stiff as in pain,
Having been overturned with an angry crack;
And there till morning, alas, it must remain.

On the terrace
No blood-trace,
No sorry glitter
Of a knife, nothing:
Not even the fine-torn fragments of a letter
Or the dull gleam of a flung-off wedding-ring.

Still stable
On the table
Two long-stemmed glasses,
One full of drink,
Watch how the rat among the vines passes
And how the moon trembles on the crag's brink.

Grotesques

I

My Chinese uncle, gouty, deaf, half-blinded,
And more than a trifle absent-minded,
Astonished all St James's Square one day
By giving long and unexceptionably exact directions
To a little coolie girl, who'd lost her way.

II

The Lion-faced Boy at the Fair
And the Heir Apparent
Were equally slow at remembering people's faces.

But whenever they met, incognito, in the Brazilian
Pavilion, the Row and such-like places,
They exchanged, it is said, their sternest nods –
Like gods of dissimilar races.

III

Dr Newman with the crooked pince-nez
Had studied in Vienna and Chicago.
Chess was his only relaxation.
And Dr Newman remained unperturbed
By every nastier manifestation
Of pluto-democratic civilization:
All that was cranky, corny, ill-behaved,
Unnecessary, askew or orgiastic
Would creep unbidden to his side-door (hidden
Behind a poster in the Tube Station,
Nearly half-way up the moving-stairs),
Push its way in, to squat there undisturbed
Among box-files and tubular steel-chairs.
He was once seen at the Philharmonic Hall
Noting the reactions of two patients,
With pronounced paranoiac tendencies,
To old Dutch music. He appeared to recall
A tin of lozenges in his breast-pocket,
Put his hand confidently in –
And drew out a black imp, or sooterkin,
Six inches long, with one ear upside-down,
Licking at a vanilla ice-cream cornet –
Then put it back again with a slight frown.

IV

A Royal Duke, with no campaigning medals
To dignify his Orders, he would speak
Nostalgically at times of Mozambique

Where once the ship he cruised in ran aground:
How he drank cocoa, from a sailor's mug,
Poured from the common jug,
While loyal toasts went round.

V

Sir John addressed the Snake God in his temple,
Which was full of bats, not as a votary
But with the somewhat cynical courtesy,
Just short of condescension,
He might have paid the Governor-General
Of a small, hot, backward colony.
He was well versed in primitive religion,
But found this an embarrassing occasion:
The God was immense, noisy and affable,
Began to tickle him with a nervous chuckle,
Unfobbed a great gold clock for him to listen,
Hissed like a snake, and swallowed him at one
    mouthful.

VI

All horses on the racecourse of Tralee
    Have four more legs in gallop than in trot –
    Two pairs fully extended, two pairs not;
And yet no thoroughbred with either three
    Or five legs but is mercilessly shot.
I watched a filly gnaw her fifth leg free,
Warned by a speaking mare since turned silentiary.

The Survivor

To die with a forlorn hope, but soon to be raised
By hags, the spoilers of the field, to elude their claws
And stand once more on a well-swept parade-ground,

Scarred and bemedalled, sword upright in fist
At head of a new undaunted company:

Is this joy? to be doubtless alive again,
And the others dead? Will your nostrils gladly savour
The fragrance, always new, of a first hedge-rose?
Will your ears be charmed by the thrush's melody
Sung as though he had himself devised it?

And is this joy: after the double suicide
(Heart against heart) to be restored entire,
To smooth your hair and wash away the life-blood,
And presently seek a young and innocent bride,
Whispering in the dark: 'for ever and ever'?

Beauty in Trouble

Beauty in trouble flees to the good angel
   On whom she can rely
To pay her cab-fare, run a steaming bath,
   Poultice her bruised eye;

Will not at first, whether for shame or caution,
   Her difficulty disclose;
Until he draws a cheque book from his plumage,
   Asking how much she owes;

(Breakfast in bed: coffee and marmalade,
   Toast, eggs, orange-juice,
After a long, sound sleep – the first since when? –
   And no word of abuse.)

Loves him less only than her saint-like mother,
   Promises to repay
His loans and most seraphic thoughtfulness
   A million-fold one day.

Beauty grows plump, renews her broken courage
  And, borrowing ink and pen,
Writes a news-letter to the evil angel
  (Her first gay act since when?):

The fiend who beats, betrays and sponges on her,
  Persuades her white is black,
Flaunts vespertilian wing and cloven hoof;
  And soon will fetch her back.

Virtue, good angel, is its own reward:
  Your guineas were well spent.
But would you to the marriage of true minds
  Admit impediment?

Sirocco at Deyá

How most unnatural-seeming, yet how proper:
The sea like a cat with fur rubbed the wrong way,
As the sirocco with its furnace flavour
Dashes at full tilt around the village
['From every-which-a-way, hot as a two-buck pistol']
Stripping green olives from the blown-back boughs,
Scorching the roses, blinding the eyes with sand;
While slanderous tongues in the small cafés
And in the tightly-shuttered limestone houses
Clack defamation, incite and invite
Knives to consummate their near-murders . . .
Look up, a great grey cloud broods nonchalant
On the mountain-top nine hundred feet above us,
Motionless and turgid, blotting out the sun,
And from it sneers a supercilious Devil:
'Mere local wind: no messenger of mine!'

Your Private Way

Whether it was your way of walking
Or of laughing moved me,
At sight of you a song wavered
Ghostly on my lips; I could not voice it,
Uncertain what the notes or key.

Be thankful I am no musician,
Sweet Anonymity, to madden you
With your own private walking-laughing way
Imitated on a beggar's fiddle
Or blared across the square on All Fools' Day.

The White Goddess

All saints revile her, and all sober men
Ruled by the God Apollo's golden mean –
In scorn of which we sailed to find her
In distant regions likeliest to hold her
Whom we desired above all things to know,
Sister of the mirage and echo.

It was a virtue not to stay,
To go our headstrong and heroic way
Seeking her out at the volcano's head,
Among pack ice, or where the track had faded
Beyond the cavern of the seven sleepers:
Whose broad high brow was white as any leper's,
Whose eyes were blue, with rowan-berry lips,
With hair curled honey-coloured to white hips.

The sap of Spring in the young wood a-stir
Will celebrate with green the Mother,
And every song-bird shout awhile for her;
But we are gifted, even in November
Rawest of seasons, with so huge a sense
Of her nakedly worn magnificence
We forget cruelty and past betrayal,
Heedless of where the next bright bolt may fall.

The Song of Blodeuwedd
(from the mediaeval Welsh)

Not of father nor of mother
Was my blood, was my body.
I was spellbound by Gwydion,
Prime enchanter of the Britons,
When he formed me from nine blossoms,
    Nine buds of various kind:
From primrose of the mountain,
Broom, meadow-sweet and cockle,
    Together intertwined,
From the bean in its shade bearing
A white spectral army
    Of earth, of earthy kind,
From blossoms of the nettle,
Oak, thorn and bashful chestnut –
Nine powers of nine flowers,
    Nine powers in me combined,
        Nine buds of plant and tree.
Long and white are my fingers
        As the ninth wave of the sea.

Instructions to the Orphic Adept

[In part translated from the Timpone Grande and
Compagno Orphic tablets.]

So soon as ever your mazed spirit descends
From daylight into darkness, Man, remember
What you have suffered here in Samothrace,
What you have suffered.

After your passage through Hell's seven floods,
Whose fumes of sulphur will have parched your
    throat,
The Halls of Judgement shall loom up before you,
A miracle of jasper and of onyx.
To the left hand there bubbles a black spring
Overshadowed with a great white cypress.
Avoid this spring, which is Forgetfulness;
Though all the common rout rush down to drink,
Avoid this spring.

To the right hand there lies a secret pool
Alive with speckled trout and fish of gold;
A hazel overshadows it. Ophion,
Primaeval serpent straggling in the branches,
Darts out his tongue. This holy pool is fed
By dripping water; guardians stand before it.
Run to this pool, the pool of Memory,
Run to this pool.

Then will the guardians scrutinize you, saying:
'Who are you, who? What have you to remember?
Do you not fear Ophion's flickering tongue?
Go rather to the spring beneath the cypress,
Flee from this pool.'

Then you shall answer: 'I am parched with thirst.
Give me to drink. I am a child of Earth,
But of Sky also, come from Samothrace.
Witness the glint of amber on my brow.
Out of the Pure I come, as you may see.
I also am of your thrice-blessed kin,
Child of the three-fold Queen of Samothrace;
Have made full quittance for my deeds of blood,
Have been by her invested in sea-purple,
And like a kid have fallen into milk,
Give me to drink, now I am parched with thirst,
Give me to drink!'

But they will ask you yet: 'What of your feet?'
You shall reply: 'My feet have borne me here
Out of the weary wheel, the circling years,
To that still, spokeless wheel: – Persephone.
Give me to drink!'

Then they will welcome you with fruit and flowers,
And lead you toward the ancient dripping hazel,
Crying: 'Brother of our immortal blood,
Drink and remember glorious Samothrace!'
Then you shall drink.

You shall drink deep of that refreshing draught,
To become lords of the uninitiated
Twittering ghosts, Hell's countless populace –
To become heroes, knights upon swift horses,
Pronouncing oracles from tall white tombs
By the nymphs tended. They with honey water
Shall pour libations to your serpent shapes,
That you may drink.

Lament for Pasiphaë

Dying sun, shine warm a little longer!
My eye, dazzled with tears, shall dazzle yours,
Conjuring you to shine and not to move.
You, sun, and I all afternoon have laboured
Beneath a dewless and oppressive cloud –
A fleece now gilded with our common grief
That this must be a night without a moon.
Dying sun, shine warm a little longer!

Faithless she was not: she was very woman,
Smiling with dire impartiality,
Sovereign, with heart unmatched, adored of men,
Until Spring's cuckoo with bedraggled plumes
Tempted her pity and her truth betrayed.
Then she who shone for all resigned her being,
And this must be a night without a moon.
Dying sun, shine warm a little longer!

Counting the Beats

You, love, and I,
(He whispers) you and I,
And if no more than only you and I
What care you or I?

Counting the beats,
Counting the slow heart beats,
The bleeding to death of time in slow heart beats,
Wakeful they lie.

Cloudless day,
Night, and a cloudless day;
Yet the huge storm will burst upon their heads one day
From a bitter sky.

Where shall we be,
(She whispers) where shall we be,
When death strikes home, O where then shall we be
Who were you and I?

Not there but here,
(He whispers) only here,
As we are, here, together, now and here,
Always you and I.

Counting the beats,
Counting the slow heart beats,
The bleeding to death of time in slow heart beats,
Wakeful they lie.

Questions in a Wood

The parson to his pallid spouse,
    The hangman to his whore,
Do both not mumble the same vows,
    Both knock at the same door?

And when the fury of their knocks
    Has waned, and that was that,
What answer comes, unless the pox
    Or one more parson's brat?

Tell me, my love, my flower of flowers,
    True woman to this man,
What have their deeds to do with ours
    Or any we might plan?

Your startled gaze, your restless hand,
    Your hair like Thames in flood,
And choked voice, battling to command
    The insurgence of your blood:

How can they spell the dark word said
    Ten thousand times a night
By women as corrupt and dead
    As you are proud and bright?

And how can I, in the same breath,
    Though warned against the cheat,
Vilely deliver love to death
    Wrapped in a rumpled sheet?

Yet, if from delicacy of pride
    We choose to hold apart,
Will no blue hag appear, to ride
    Hell's wager in each heart?

Darien

It is a poet's privilege and fate
To fall enamoured of the one Muse
Who variously haunts this island earth.

She was your mother, Darien,
And presaged by the darting halcyon bird
Would run green-sleeved along her ridges,
Treading the asphodels and heather-trees
With white feet bare.

Often at moonrise I had watched her go,
And a cold shudder shook me
To see the curved blaze of her Cretan axe.

Averted her set face, her business
Not yet with me, long-striding,
She would ascend the peak and pass from sight.
But once at full moon, by the sea's verge,
I came upon her without warning.

Unrayed she stood, with long hair streaming,
A cockle-shell cupped in her warm hands,
Her axe propped idly on a stone.

No awe possessed me, only a great grief;
Wanly she smiled, but would not lift her eyes
(As a young girl will greet the stranger).
I stood upright, a head taller than she.
'See who has come,' said I.

She answered: 'If I lift my eyes to yours
And our eyes marry, man, what then?
Will they engender my son Darien?
Swifter than wind, with straight and nut-brown
    hair,
Tall, slender-shanked, grey-eyed, untameable;
Never was born, nor ever will be born
A child to equal my son Darien,
Guardian of the hid treasures of your world.'

I knew then by the trembling of her hands
For whom that flawless blade would sweep:
My own oracular head, swung by its hair.

'Mistress,' I cried, 'the times are evil
And you have charged me with their remedy.
O, where my head is now, let nothing be
But a clay counterfeit with nacre blink:
Only look up, so Darien may be born.

'He is the northern star, the spell of knowledge,
Pride of all hunters and all fishermen,
Your deathless fawn, an eaglet of your eyrie,
The topmost branch of your unfellable tree,
A tear streaking the summer night,
The new green of my hope.'
                                    Lifting her eyes,
She held mine for a lost eternity.
'Sweetheart,' said I, 'strike now, for Darien's sake!'

The Portrait

She speaks always in her own voice
Even to strangers; but those other women
Exercise their borrowed, or false, voices
Even on sons and daughters.

She can walk invisibly at noon
Along the high road; but those other women
Gleam phosphorescent – broad hips and gross
    fingers –
Down every lampless alley.

She is wild and innocent, pledged to love
Through all disaster; but those other women
Decry her for a witch or a common drab
And glare back when she greets them.

Here is her portrait, gazing sidelong at me,
The hair in disarray, the young eyes pleading:
'And you, love? As unlike those other men
As I those other women?'

Prometheus

Close bound in a familiar bed
All night I tossed, rolling my head;
Now dawn returns in vain, for still
The vulture squats on her warm hill.

I am in love as giants are
That dote upon the evening star,
And this lank bird is come to prove
The intractability of love.

Yet still, with greedy eye half shut,
Rend the raw liver from its gut:
Feed, jealousy, do not fly away –
If she who fetched you also stay.

The Straw

Peace, the wild valley streaked with torrents,
A hoopoe perched on his warm rock. Then why
This tremor of the straw between my fingers?

What should I fear? Have I not testimony
In her own hand, signed with her own name
That my love fell as lightning on her heart?

These questions, bird, are not rhetorical.
Watch how the straw twitches and leaps
As though the earth quaked at a distance.

Requited love; but better unrequited
If this chance instrument gives warning
Of cataclysmic anguish far away.

Were she at ease, warmed by the thought of me,
Would not my hand stay steady as this rock?
Have I undone her by my vehemence?

Dialogue on the Headland

SHE: You'll not forget these rocks and what I told you?
HE: How could I? Never: whatever happens.
SHE: What do you think might happen?
    Might you fall out of love? – did you mean that?
HE: Never, never! 'Whatever' was a sop
    For jealous listeners in the shadows.
SHE: You haven't answered me. I asked:
    'What do you think might happen?'
HE: Whatever happens: though the skies should fall
    Raining their larks and vultures in our laps –
SHE: 'Though the seas turn to slime' – say that –
    'Though water-snakes be hatched with six heads.'
HE: Though the seas turn to slime, or tower
    In an arching wave above us, three miles high –
SHE: 'Though she should break with you' – dare you say
        that? –
    'Though she deny her words on oath.'
HE: I had that in mind to say, or nearly;
    It hurt so much I choked it back.
SHE: How many other days can't you forget?
    How many other loves and landscapes?
HE: You are jealous?
HE: Damnably.
SHE: The past is past.
HE: And this?
SHE: Whatever happens, this goes on.

125

SHE: Without a future? Sweetheart, tell me now:
     What do you want of me? I must know that.
HE: Nothing that isn't freely mine already.
SHE: Say what is freely yours and you shall have it.
HE: Nothing that, loving you, I could dare take.
SHE: O, for an answer with no 'nothing' in it!
HE: Then give me everything that's left.
SHE: Left after what?
HE: After whatever happens:
     Skies have already fallen, seas are slime,
     Watersnakes poke and peer six-headedly –
SHE: And I lie snugly in the Devil's arms.
HE: I said: 'Whatever happens.' Are you crying?
SHE: You'll not forget me – ever, ever, ever?

A Lost Jewel

Who on your breast pillows his head now,
Jubilant to have won
The heart beneath on fire for him alone,

At dawn will hear you, plagued by nightmare,
Mumble and weep
About some blue jewel you were sworn to keep.

Wake, blink, laugh out in reassurance,
Yet your tears will say:
'It was not mine to lose or give away.

'For love it shone – never for the madness
Of a strange bed –
Light on my finger, fortune in my head.'

Roused by your naked grief and beauty,
For lust he will burn:
'Turn to me, sweetheart! Why do you not turn?'

The Sea Horse

Since now in every public place
Lurk phantoms who assume your walk and face,
You cannot yet have utterly abjured me
Nor stifled the insistent roar of the sea.

Do as I do: confide your unquiet love
(For one who never owed you less than love)
To this indomitable hippocamp,
Child of your element, coiled-a-ramp,
Having ridden out worse tempests than you know of;
Under his horny ribs a blood-red stain
Portends the renewal of our pain.
Sweetheart, make much of him and shed
Tears on his taciturn dry head.

Cat-Goddesses

A perverse habit of cat-goddesses –
Even the blackest of them, black as coals
Save for a new moon blazing on each breast,
With coral tongues and beryl eyes like lamps,
Long-leggèd, pacing three by three in nines –
This obstinate habit is to yield themselves,
In verisimilar love-ecstasies,
To tatter-eared and slinking alley-toms
No less below the common run of cats
Than they above it; which they do for spite,
To provoke jealousy – not the least abashed
By such gross-headed, rabbit-coloured litters
As soon they shall be happy to desert.

The Blue-Fly

Five summer days, five summer nights,
The ignorant, loutish, giddy blue-fly
Hung without motion on the cling peach,
Humming occasionally: 'O my love, my fair one!'
    As in the *Canticles*.

Magnified one thousand times, the insect
Looks farcically human; laugh if you will!
Bald head, stage-fairy wings, blear eyes,
A caved-in chest, hairy black mandibles,
    Long spindly thighs.

The crime was detected on the sixth day.
What then could be said or done? By anyone?
It would have been vindictive, mean and what-not
To swat that fly for being a blue-fly,
    For debauch of a peach.

Is it fair, either, to bring a microscope
To bear on the case, even in search of truth?
Nature, doubtless, has some compelling cause
To glut the carriers of her epidemics –
    Nor did the peach complain.

The Window Sill

Presage and caveat not only seem
To come in dream
But do so come in dream.

When the cock crew and phantoms floated by,
This dreamer I
Out of the house went I,

Down long unsteady streets to a queer square;
And who was there,
Or whom did I know there?

Julia, leaning on her window sill.
'I love you still,'
Said she, 'O love me still!'

I answered: 'Julia, do you love me best?'
'What of this breast,'
She mourned, 'this flowery breast?'

Then a wild sobbing spread from door to door,
And every floor
Cried shame on every floor,

As she unlaced her bosom to disclose
Each breast a rose,
A white and cankered rose.

Spoils

When all is over and you march for home,
The spoils of war are easily disposed of:
Standards, weapons of combat, helmets, drums
May decorate a staircase or a study,
While lesser gleanings of the battlefield –
Coins, watches, wedding-rings, gold teeth and such –
Are sold anonymously for solid cash.

The spoils of love present a different case,
When all is over and you march for home:

That lock of hair, these letters and the portrait
May not be publicly displayed; nor sold;
Nor burned; nor returned (the heart being obstinate) –
Yet never dare entrust them to a safe
For fear they burn a hole through two-foot steel.

Rhea

On her shut lids the lightning flickers,
Thunder explodes above her bed,
An inch from her lax arm the rain hisses;
Discrete she lies,

Not dead but entranced, dreamlessly
With slow breathing, her lips curved
In a half-smile archaic, her breast bare,
Hair astream.

The house rocks, a flood suddenly rising
Bears away bridges: oak and ash
Are shivered to the roots – royal green timber.
She nothing cares.

(Divine Augustus, trembling at the storm,
Wrapped sealskin on his thumb; divine Gaius
Made haste to hide himself in a deep cellar,
Distraught by fear.)

Rain, thunder, lightning: pretty children.
'Let them play,' her mother-mind repeats;
'They do no harm, unless from high spirits
Or by mishap.'

Gratitude for a Nightmare

His appearances are incalculable,
His strength terrible,
I do not know his name.

Huddling pensive for weeks on end, he
Gives only random hints of life, such as
Strokes of uncomfortable coincidence.

To eat heartily, dress warmly, lie snugly
And earn respect as a leading citizen
Granted long credit at all shops and inns –

How dangerous! I had feared this shag demon
Would not conform with my conformity
And in some leaner belly makes his lair.

But now in dream he suddenly bestrides me. . . .
'All's well' I groan, and fumble for a light,
Brow bathed in sweat, heart pounding.

The Naked and the Nude

For me, the naked and the nude
(By lexicographers construed
As synonyms that should express
The same deficiency of dress
Or shelter) stand as wide apart
As love from lies, or truth from art.

Lovers without reproach will gaze
On bodies naked and ablaze;

The Hippocratic eye will see
In nakedness, anatomy;
And naked shines the Goddess when
She mounts her lion among men.

The nude are bold, the nude are sly
To hold each treasonable eye.
While draping by a showman's trick
Their dishabille in rhetoric,
They grin a mock-religious grin
Of scorn at those of naked skin.

The naked, therefore, who compete
Against the nude may know defeat;
Yet when they both together tread
The briary pastures of the dead,
By Gorgons with long whips pursued,
How naked go the sometime nude!

A Slice of Wedding Cake

Why have such scores of lovely, gifted girls
    Married impossible men?
Simple, self-sacrifice may be ruled out,
    And missionary endeavour, nine times out of ten.

Repeat 'impossible men'; not merely rustic
    Foul-tempered or depraved
(Dramatic foils chosen to show the world
    How well women behave, and always have behaved).

Impossible men: idle, illiterate,
   Self-pitying, dirty, sly,
For whose appearance even in City parks
   Excuses must be made to casual passers-by.

Has God's supply of tolerable husbands
   Fallen, in fact, so low?
Or do I always over-value woman
   At the expense of man?
                Do I?
                      It might be so.

Call It a Good Marriage

Call it a good marriage –
For no one ever questioned
Her warmth, his masculinity,
Their interlocking views;
Except one stray graphologist
Who frowned in speculation
At her h's and her s's,
His p's and w's.

Though few would still subscribe
To the monogamic axiom
That strife below the hip-bones
Need not estrange the heart,
Call it a good marriage:
More drew those two together,
Despite a lack of children,
Than pulled them apart.

Call it a good marriage:
They never fought in public,

They acted circumspectly
And faced the world with pride;
Thus the hazards of their love-bed
Were none of our damned business –
Till as jurymen we sat on
Two deaths by suicide.

Around the Mountain

Some of you may know, others perhaps can guess
    How it is to walk all night through summer rain
(Thin rain that shrouds a beneficent full moon),
    To circle a mountain, and then limp home again.

The experience varies with a traveller's age
    And bodily strength, and strength of the love affair
That harries him out of doors in steady drizzle,
    With neither jacket nor hat, and holds him there.

Still, let us concede some common elements:
    Wild-fire that, until midnight, burns his feet;
And surging rankly up, strong on the palate,
    Scents of July, imprisoned by long heat.

Add: the sub-human, black tree-silhouettes
    Against a featureless pale pall of sky;
Unseen, gurgling water; the bulk and menace
    Of entranced houses; a wraith wandering by.

Milestones, each one witness of a new mood –
    Anger, desperation, grief, regret;
Her too-familiar face that whirls and totters
    In memory, never willing to stay set.

Whoever makes the desired turning-point,
  Which means another fifteen miles to go,
Learns more from dawn than love, so far, has taught
    him;
  Especially the false dawn, when cocks first crow.

Those last few miles are easy: being assured
  Of the fact, why should he fabricate fresh lies?
His house looms up; the eaves drip drowsily;
  The windows blaze to a resolute sunrise.

The Face in the Mirror

Grey haunted eyes, absent-mindedly glaring
From wide, uneven orbits; one brow drooping
Somewhat over the eye
Because of a missile fragment still inhering,
Skin deep, as a foolish record of old-world fighting.

Crookedly broken nose – low tackling caused it;
Cheeks, furrowed; coarse grey hair, flying frenetic;
Forehead, wrinkled and high;
Jowls, prominent; ears, large; jaw, pugilistic;
Teeth, few; lips, full and ruddy; mouth, ascetic.

I pause with razor poised, scowling derision
At the mirrored man whose beard needs my attention,
And once more ask him why
He still stands ready, with a boy's presumption,
To court the queen in her high silk pavilion.

Symptoms of Love

Love is a universal migraine,
A bright stain on the vision
Blotting out reason.

Symptoms of true love
Are leanness, jealousy,
Laggard dawns;

Are omens and nightmares –
Listening for a knock,
Waiting for a sign:

For a touch of her fingers
In a darkened room,
For a searching look.

Take courage, lover!
Could you endure such grief
At any hand but hers?

The Visitation

Drowsing in my chair of disbelief
I watch the door as it slowly opens –
A trick of the night wind?

Your slender body seems a shaft of moonlight
Against the door as it gently closes.
Do you cast no shadow?

Your whisper is too soft for credence,
Your tread like blossom drifting from a bough,
Your touch even softer.

You wear that sorrowful and tender mask
Which on high mountain tops in heather-flow
Entrances lonely shepherds;

And though a single word scatters all doubts
I quake for wonder at your choice of me:
Why, why and why?

Troughs of Sea

'Do you delude yourself?' a neighbour asks,
Dismayed by my abstraction.
But though love cannot question love
Nor need deny its need,

Pity the man who finds a rebel heart
Under his breastbone drumming
Which reason warns him he should drown
In midnight wastes of sea.

Now as he stalks between tormented pines
(The moon in her last quarter)
A lissom spectre glides ahead
And utters not a word.

Waves tasselled with dark weed come rearing up
Like castle waves, disclosing
Deep in their troughs a ribbed sea-floor
To break his bones upon.

– Clasp both your hands under my naked foot
And press hard, as I taught you:
A trick to mitigate the pangs
Either of birth or love.

The Starred Coverlet

A difficult achievement for true lovers
Is to lie mute, without embrace or kiss,
Without a rustle or a smothered sigh,
Basking each in the other's glory.

Let us not undervalue lips or arms
As reassurances of constancy,
Or speech as necessary communication
When troubled hearts go groping through the
    dusk;

Yet lovers who have learned this last
    refinement –
To lie apart, yet sleep and dream together
Motionless under their starred coverlet –
Crown love with wreaths of myrtle.

Turn of the Moon

Never forget who brings the rain
In swarthy goatskin bags from a far sea:
It is the Moon as she turns, repairing
Damages of long drought and sunstroke.

Never count upon rain, never foretell it,
For no power can bring rain
Except the Moon as she turns; and who can rule her?

She is prone to delay the necessary floods,
Lest such a gift might become obligation,
A month, or two, or three; then suddenly
Not relenting but by way of whim
Will perhaps conjure from the cloudless west
A single rain-drop to surprise with hope
Each haggard, upturned face.

Were the Moon a Sun, we would count upon her
To bring rain seasonably as she turned;
Yet no one thinks to thank the regular Sun
For shining fierce in summer, mild in winter –
Why should the Moon so drudge?

But if one night she brings us, as she turns,
Soft, steady, even, copious rain
That harms no leaf nor flower, but gently falls
Hour after hour, sinking to the tap roots,
And the sodden earth exhales at dawn
A long sigh scented with pure gratitude,
Such rain – the first rain of our lives, it seems,
Neither foretold, cajoled, nor counted on –
Is woman giving as she loves.

Seldom Yet Now

Seldom yet now: the quality
Of this wild love between us –
Seldom the encounter,

The presence always,
Free of oath or promise.

And if we were not so
But birds of similar plumage caged
In the peace of every day,
Would we still conjure wildfire up
From common earth, as now?

Apple Island

Though cruel seas like mountains fill the bay,
Wrecking the quayside huts,
Salting our vineyards with tall showers of spray;

And though the moon shines dangerously clear,
Fixed in another cycle
Than the sun's progress round the felloe'd year;

And though I may not hope to dwell apart
With you on Apple Island
Unless my breast be docile to the dart –

Why should I fear your element, the sea,
Or the full moon, your mirror,
Or the halved apple from your holy tree?

Horizon

On a clear day how thin the horizon
Drawn between sea and sky,
Between sea-love and sky-love;

And after sunset how debatable
Even for an honest eye.

'Do as you will tonight,'
Said she, and so he did
By moonlight, candlelight,
Candlelight and moonlight,
While pillowed clouds the horizon hid.

Knowing-not-knowing that such deeds must
    end
In a curse which lovers long past weeping for
Had heaped upon him: she would be gone one
    night
With his familiar friend,
Granting him leave her beauty to explore
By moonlight, candlelight,
Candlelight and moonlight.

I'd Die for You

I'd die for you, or you for me,
So furious is our jealousy –
And if you doubt this to be true
Kill me outright, lest I kill you.

The Wreath

A bitter year it was. What woman ever
Cared for me so, yet so ill-used me,
Came in so close and drew so far away,

So much promised and performed so little,
So murderously her own love dared betray?
Since I can never be clear out of your debt,
Queen of ingratitude, to my dying day,
You shall be punished with a deathless crown
For your dark head, resist it how you may.

Lion Lover

You chose a lion to be your lover –
Me, who in joy such doom greeting
Dared jealously undertake
Cruel ordeals long foreseen and known,
Springing a trap baited with flesh: my own.

Nor would I now exchange this lion heart
For a less furious other,
Though by the Moon possessed
I gnaw at dry bones in a lost lair
And, when clouds cover her, roar my despair.

Gratitude and affection I disdain
As cheap in any market:
Your naked feet upon my scarred shoulders,
Your eyes naked with love,
Are all the gifts my beasthood can approve.

In Her Praise

This they know well: the Goddess yet abides.
Though each new lovely woman whom she rides,
Straddling her neck a year or two or three,
Should sink beneath such weight of majesty

And, groping back to humankind, gainsay
The headlong power that whitened all her way
With a broad track of trefoil – leaving you,
Her chosen lover, ever again thrust through
With daggers, your purse rifled, your rings gone –
Nevertheless they call you to live on
To parley with the pure, oracular dead,
To hear the wild pack whimpering overhead,
To watch the moon tugging at her cold tides.
Woman is mortal woman. She abides.

A Restless Ghost

Alas for obstinate doubt: the dread
Of error in supposing my heart freed,
All care for her stone dead!
Ineffably will shine the hills and radiant coast
Of early morning when she is gone indeed,
Her divine elements disbanded, disembodied
And through the misty orchards in love spread –
When she is gone indeed –
But still among them moves her restless ghost.

Beware, Madam!

Beware, madam, of the witty devil,
The arch intriguer who walks disguised
In a poet's cloak, his gay tongue oozing evil.

Would you be a Muse? He will so declare you,
Pledging his blind allegiance,
Yet remain secret and uncommitted.

Poets are men: are single-hearted lovers
Who adore and trust beyond all reason,
Who die honourably at the gates of hell.

The Muse alone is licensed to do murder
And to betray: weeping with honest tears
She thrones each victim in her paradise.

But from this Muse the devil borrows an art
That ill becomes a man. Beware, madam:
He plots to strip you bare of woman-pride.

He is capable of seducing your twin-sister
On the same pillow, and neither she nor you
Will suspect the act, so close a glamour he sheds.

Alas, being honourably single-hearted,
You adore and trust beyond all reason,
Being no more a Muse than he a poet.

Hedges Freaked with Snow

No argument, no anger, no remorse,
    No dividing of blame.
There was poison in the cup – why should we ask
    From whose hand it came?

No grief for our dead love, no howling gales
    That through darkness blow,
But the smile of sorrow, a wan winter landscape,
    Hedges freaked with snow.

In Time

In time all undertakings are made good,
All cruelties remedied,
Each bond resealed more firmly than before –
Befriend us, Time, Love's gaunt executor!

She is No Liar

She is no liar, yet she will wash away
Honey from her lips, blood from her shadowy
  hand,
And, dressed at dawn in clean white robes will
  say,
Trusting the ignorant world to understand:
'Such things no longer are; this is today.'

A Last Poem

A last poem, and a very last, and yet another –
O, when can I give over?
Must I drive the pen until blood bursts from my
  nails
And my breath fails and I shake with fever,
Or sit well wrapped in a many-coloured cloak
Where the moon shines new through Castle
  Crystal?
Shall I never hear her whisper softly:
'But this is truth written by you only,
And for me only; therefore, love, have done'?

To Beguile and Betray

To beguile and betray, though pardonable in
  women,
Slowly quenches the divine need-fire
By true love kindled in them. Have you not
  watched
The immanent Goddess fade from their brows
When they make private to her mysteries
Some whip-scarred rogue from the hulks, some
  painted clown
From the pantomime – and afterwards accuse you
Of jealous hankering for the mandalot
Rather than horror and sick foreboding
That she will never return to the same house?

I Will Write

He had done for her all that a man could,
And, some might say, more than a man should.
Then was ever a flame so recklessly blown out
Or a last goodbye so negligent as this?
'I will write to you,' she muttered briefly,
Tilting her cheek for a polite kiss;
Then walked away, nor ever turned about. . . .

Long letters written and mailed in her own head –
There are no mails in a city of the dead.

Bird of Paradise

At sunset, only to his true love,
The bird of paradise opened wide his wings
Displaying emerald plumage shot with gold
Unguessed even by him.
                              True, that wide crest
Had blazoned royal estate, and the tropic flowers
Through which he flew had shown example
Of what brave colours gallantry might flaunt,
But these were other. She asked herself,
   trembling:
'What did I do to awake such glory?'

Song: Sword and Rose

The King of Hearts a broadsword bears,
   The Queen of Hearts, a rose –
Though why, not every gambler cares
   Or cartomancer knows.

Be beauty yours, be honour mine,
   Yet word and rose are one:
Great emblems that in love combine
   Until the dealing's done;

For no card, whether small or face,
   Shall overtrump our two
Except that Heart of Hearts, the Ace,
   To which their title's due.

Bats at play taunt us with 'guess how many',
And music sounds far off, tempered by sea.
Above the edge of doom sits woman
Communing with herself. 'Dear love,' says she,
As it were apostrophizing cat or dog,
'Sometimes by a delicate glance and gesture
You almost seem to understand me,
Poor honest creature of the blue eyes,
Having crept closer to my sealed bosom
With your more desperate faith in womankind
Than any other since I first flowered.

It may be best you cannot read my mind.'

The Green Castle

The first heaven is a flowery plain;
The second, a glass mountain;
The third, likewise terrestrial,
Is an orchard-close unclouded
By prescience of death or change
Or the blood-sports of desire:
Our childhood paradise.

The next three heavens, known as celestial,
Are awkward of approach.
Mind is the prudent rider; body, the ass
Disciplined always by a harsh bit,
Accepts his daily diet of thorns

And frugal, brackish water;
Holds converse with archangels.

The seventh heaven, most unlike those others,
We once contrived to enter
By a trance of love; it is a green castle
Girdled with ramparts of blue sea
And silent but for the waves' leisured wash.
There Adam rediscovered Eve:
She wrapped him in her arms.

Not to Sleep

Not to sleep all the night long, for pure joy,
Counting no sheep and careless of chimes,
Welcoming the dawn confabulation
Of birds, her children, who discuss idly
Fanciful details of the promised coming –
Will she be wearing red, or russet, or blue,
Or pure white? – whatever she wears, glorious:
Not to sleep all the night long, for pure joy,
This is given to few but at last to me,
So that when I laugh and stretch and leap from bed
I shall glide downstairs, my feet brushing the
    carpet
In courtesy to civilized progression,
Though, did I wish, I could soar through the
    open window
And perch on a branch above, acceptable ally
Of the birds still alert, grumbling gently
    together.

Whole Love

Every choice is always the wrong choice,
Every vote cast is always cast away –
How can truth hover between alternatives?

Then love me more than dearly, love me wholly,
Love me with no weighing of circumstance,
As I am pledged in honour to love you:

With no weakness, with no speculation
On what might happen should you and I prove
    less
Than bringers-to-be of our own certainty.
Neither was born by hazard: each foreknew
The extreme possession we are grown into.

The Impossible

Dear love, since the impossible proves
    Our sole recourse from this distress,
Claim it: the ebony ritual-mask of no
    Cannot outstare a living yes.

Claim it without despond or hate
    Or greed; but in your gentler tone
Say: 'This is ours, the impossible,' and silence
    Will give consent it is ours alone.

The impossible has wild-cat claws
    Which you would rather meet and die
Than commit love to time's curative venom
    And break our oath; for so would I.

Iron Palace

We stood together, side by side, rooted
At the iron heart of circumambient hills,
Parents to a new age, weeping in awe
That the lot had fallen, of all mankind, on us
Now sealed as love's exemplars.

We could not prevaricate or argue,
Citing involvement in some alien scene,
Nor plead unworthiness: none else would
    venture
To live detached from force of circumstance
As history neared its ending.

We told no one. These were not strange dreams
Recalled at breakfast with a yawning smile,
Nor tales for children, on the verge of sleep,
Who ask no questions. Our predicament
Remained a silent burden.

We had no token or proof, and needed none
Of what we learned that day; but laughed softly
Watching our hands engage, in co-awareness
That these red hills warned us, on pain of death,
Never to disengage them.

Woman, wild and hard as the truth may be,
Nothing can circumvent it. We stand coupled
With chains, who otherwise might live apart
Conveniently paired, each with another,
And slide securely graveward.

Everywhere is Here

By this exchange of eyes, this encirclement
You of me, I of you, together we baffle
Logic no doubt, but never understanding;
And laugh instead of choking back the tears
When we say goodbye.

               Fog gathers thick about us
Yet a single careless pair of leaves, one green,
   one gold,
Whirl round and round each other skippingly
As though blown by a wind; pause and subside
In a double star, the gold above the green.

Everywhere is here, once we have shattered
The iron-bound laws of contiguity,
Blazoning love as an eagle with four wings
(Their complementary tinctures counterchanged)
That scorns to roost in any terrene crag.

Song: The Far Side of Your Moon

The far side of your moon is black,
   And glorious grows the vine;
Ask anything of me you lack,
   But only what is mine.

Yours is the great wheel of the sun,
   And yours the unclouded sky;
Then take my stars, take every one,
   But wear them openly.

Walking in splendour through the plain
  For all the world to see,
Since none alive shall view again
  The match of you and me.

Leaving the Rest Unsaid

Finis, apparent on an earlier page,
With fallen obelisk for colophon,
Must this be here repeated?

Death has been ruefully announced
And to die once is death enough,
Be sure, for any life-time.

Must the book end, as you would end it,
With testamentary appendices
And graveyard indices?

But no, I will not lay me down
To let your tearful music mar
The decent mystery of my progress.

So now, my solemn ones, leaving the rest
    unsaid,
Rising in air as on a gander's wing
At a careless comma,

Dead Hand

Grieve for the loveless, spiritless, faceless men
Without alternative but to protract
Reason's mortmain on what their hearts deny –
Themselves – and owed small courtesy beyond
The uncovered head, as when a hearse goes by.

Lure of Murder

A round moon suffocates the neighbouring stars
With greener light than sun through vine-leaves.
Awed by her ecstasy of solitude
I crouch among rocks, scanning the gulf, agape,
Whetting a knife on my horny sole.

Alas for the lure of murder, dear my love!
Could its employment purge two moon-vexed hearts
Of jealousy more formidable than death,
Then each would stab, stab, stab at secret parts
Of the other's beloved body where unknown
Zones of desire inperil full possession.

But never can mortal dagger serve to geld
This glory of ours, this loving beyond reason –
Death holds no remedy or alternative:
We are singled out to endure his lasting grudge
On the tall battlements of nightfall.

Arrears of Moonlight

My heart lies wrapped in red under your pillow,
My body wanders banished among the stars;
On one terrestrial pretext or another
You still withhold the extravagant arrears
Of moonlight that you owe us,
Though the owl whoops from a far olive branch
His brief, monotonous, night-long reminder.

What Did You Say?

She listened to his voice urgently pleading,
So captivated by his eloquence
She saw each word in its own grace and beauty
Drift like a flower down that clear-flowing brook,
And draw a wake of multicoloured bubbles.
But when he paused, intent on her reply,
She could stammer only: 'Love, what did you say?' –
As loath as ever to hold him in her arms
Naked, under the trees, until high day.

All Except Hannibal

Trapped in a dismal marsh, he told his troops:
'No lying down, lads! Form your own mess-groups
And sit in circles, each man on the knees
Of the man behind; then nobody will freeze.'

They obeyed his orders, as the cold sun set,
Drowsing all night in one another's debt,
All except Hannibal himself, who chose
His private tree-stump – he was one of those!

Stolen Jewel

You weep whole-heartedly – your shining tears
Roll down for sorrow, not like mine for joy.
Dear love, should we not scorn to treat each other
With palliatives and with placebos?

Under a blinding moon you took from me
This jewel of wonder, but unaware
That it was yielded only on condition
Of whole possession; that it still denies you
Strength or desire for its restitution.

What do you fear? My hand around your throat?
What do I fear? Your dagger through my heart?
Must we not rage alone together
In lofts of singular high starriness?

The Snapped Thread

Desire, first, by a natural miracle
United bodies, united hearts, blazed beauty;
Transcended bodies, transcended hearts.

Two souls, now unalterably one
In whole love always and for ever,
Soar out of twilight, through upper air,
Let fall their sensuous burden.

Is it kind, though, is it honest even,
To consort with none but spirits –
Leaving true-wedded hearts like ours
In enforced night-long separation,
Each to its random bodily inclination,
The thread of miracle snapped?

Ecstasy of Chaos

When the immense drugged universe explodes
In a cascade of unendurable colour
And leaves us gasping naked,
This is no more than ecstasy of chaos:
Hold fast, with both hands, to that royal love
Which alone, as we know certainly, restores
Fragmentation into true being.

Dancing Flame

Pass now in metaphor beyond birds,
Their seasonal nesting and migration,
Their airy gambols, their repetitive song;
Beyond the puma and the ocelot
That spring in air and follow us with their eyes;
Beyond all creatures but our own selves,
Eternal genii of dancing flame
Armed with the irreproachable secret
Of love, which is: never to turn back.

Birth of Angels

Never was so profound a shadow thrown
On earth as by your sun: a black roundel
Harbouring an unheard-of generation
Fledged by the sun ablaze above your own –
Wild beyond words, yet each of them an angel.

Fortunate Child

For fear strangers might intrude upon us
You and I played at being strangers,
But lent our act such verisimilitude
That when at last, by hazard, we met alone
In a secret glen where the badger earths
We had drawn away from love: did not prepare
For melting of eyes into hearts of flowers,
For sun-aureoled enhancement of hair,
For over-riding of death on an eagle's back –
Yet so it was: sky shuddered apart before us
Until, from a cleft of more than light, we both
Overheard the laugh of a fortunate child
Swung from those eagle talons in a gold cloth.

Loving True, Flying Blind

How often have I said before
That no soft 'if', no 'either-or',
Can keep my obdurate male mind
From loving true and flying blind? –

Which, though deranged beyond all cure
Of temporal reasons, know for sure
That timeless magic first began
When woman bared her soul to man.

Be bird, be blossom, comet, star,
Be paradisal gates ajar,
But still, as woman, bear you must
With who alone endures your trust.

The Near Eclipse

Out shines again the glorious round sun –
After his near-eclipse when pools of light
Thrown on the turf between leaf shadows
Grew crescent-shaped like moons – dizzying us
With paraboles of colour: regal amends
To our own sun mauled barbarously
By the same wide-mouthed dragon.

Like Owls

The blind are their own brothers; we
Form an obscure fraternity
Who, though not destitute of sight
Know ourselves doomed from birth to see,
Like owls, most clearly in half light.

On Giving

Those who dare give nothing
Are left with less than nothing;
Dear heart, you give me everything,
Which leaves you more than everything –
Though those who dare give nothing
Might judge it left you nothing.

Giving you everything,
I too, who once had nothing,
Am left with more than everything
As gifts for those with nothing
Who need, if not our everything,
At least a loving something.

In Perspective

What, keep love in *perspective?* – that old lie
Forced on the Imagination by the Eye
Which, mechanistically controlled, will tell
How rarely table-sides run parallel;
How distance shortens us; how wheels are found
Oval in shape far oftener than round;
How every ceiling-corner's out of joint;
How the broad highway tapers to a point –
Can all this fool us lovers? Not for long:
Even the blind will sense that something's wrong.

The P'eng that was a K'un
(Adapted from the Chinese of Lao Tse)

In Northern seas there roams a fish called K'un,
Of how many thousand leagues in length I know not,
Which changes to a bird called P'eng – its wing-span
Of how many thousand leagues in width I know not.
Every half-year this P'eng, that was a K'un,
Fans out its glorious feathers to the whirlwind
And soars to the most Southerly pool of Heaven.

The Finch and Sparrow, thus informed, debated:
'We by our utmost efforts may fly only
To yonder elm. How can the P'eng outdo us?
Though, indeed, neither started as a fish.'

Bower-Bird

The Bower-bird improvised a cool retreat
For the hen he honoured, doing his poor best
With parrot-plumage, orchids, bones and corals,
To engage her fancy.
              But this was no nest . . .
So, though the Penguin dropped at his hen's feet
An oval stone to signal: 'be my bride',
And though the Jackdaw's nest was glorified
With diamond rings and brooches massed inside,
It was the Bower-bird who contented me
By not equating love with matrimony.

But if that Cerberus, my mind, should be
Flung to earth by the very opiate
That frees my senses for undared adventure,
Waving them wide-eyed past me to explore
Limitless hells of disintegrity,
Endless, undifferentiatable fate
Scrolled out beyond the utter rim of nowhere,
Scrolled out . . . . . .
                  who on return fail to surrender
Their memory trophies, random wisps of horror
Trailed from my shins or tangled in my hair?

Unicorn and the White Doe

Unicorn with burning heart
Breath of love has drawn
On this desolate peak apart
At rumour of dawn,

Has trumpeted his pride
These long years mute,
Tossed his horn from side to side,
Lunged with his foot.

Like a storm of sand has run
Breaking his own boundaries,
Gone in hiding from the sun
Under camphor trees.

Straight was the course he took
Across the plain, but here with briar
And mire the tangled alleys crook,
Baulking desire.

A shoulder glistened white –
The bough still shakes –
A white doe darted out of sight
Through the forest brakes.

Tall and close the camphors grow
The grass grows thick –
Where you are I do not know,
You fly so quick.

Where have you fled from me?
I pursue, you fade,
I hunt, you hide from me
In the chequered glade.

Often from my hot lair
I would watch you drink,
A mirage of tremulous air,
At the pool's brink.

Vultures, rocking high in air
By the western gate,
Warned me with discordant cry
You are even such as I:
You have no mate.

(*1920 – recast 1966*)

A Dream of Hell

You reject the rainbow
Of our Sun castle
As hyperbolic;

You enjoin the Moon
Of our pure trysts
To condone deceit;

Lured to violence
By a lying spirit,
You break our troth.

Seven wide, enchanted
Wards of horror
Lie stretched before you,

To brand your naked breast
With impious colours,
To band your thighs.

How can I discharge
Your confused spirit
From its chosen hell?

You who once dragged me
From the bubbling slime
Of a tidal reach,

Who washed me, fed me,
Laid me in white sheets,
Warmed me in brown arms,

Would you have me cede
Our single sovereignty
To your tall demon?

Our Self

When first we came together
It was no chance foreshadowing
Of a chance happy ending.
The case grows always clearer
By its own worse disorder:
However reasonably we oppose
That unquiet integer, our self, we lose.

Perfectionists

Interalienation of their hearts
It was not, though both played resentful parts
In proud unwillingness to share
One house, one pillow, the same fare.
It was perfectionism, they confess,
To know the truth and ask for nothing less.

Their fire-eyed guardians watched from overhead:
'These two alone have learned to love,' they said,
'But neither can forget
They are not worthy of each other yet.'

The Necklace

Variegated flowers, nuts, cockle-shells
And pebbles, chosen lovingly and strung
On golden spider-webs with a gold clasp
For your neck, naturally: and each bead touched

By a child's lips as he stoops over them:
Wear these for the new miracle they announce –
All four cross-quarter-days beseech you –
Your safe return from shipwreck, drought and war,
Beautiful as before, to what you are.

Bites and Kisses

Heather and holly,
Bites and kisses,
A courtship-royal
On the hill's red cusp.
Look up, look down,
Gaze all about you –
A livelier world
By ourselves contrived:

Swan in full course
Up the Milky Way,
Moon in her wildness,
Sun ascendant
In Crab or Lion,
Beyond the bay
A pride of dolphins
Curving and tumbling
With bites and kisses . . .

Or dog-rose petals
Well-starred by dew,
Or jewelled pebbles,
Or waterlilies open
For the dragon-flies
In their silver and blue.

Spite of Mirrors

O what astonishment if you
Could see yourself as others do,
Foiling the mirror's wilful spite
That shows your left cheek as the right
And shifts your lovely crooked smile
To the wrong corner! But meanwhile
Lakes, pools and puddles all agree
(Bound in a vast conspiracy)
To reflect only your stern look
Designed for peering in a book –
No easy laugh, no glint of rage,
No thoughts in cheerful pilgrimage,
No start of guilt, no rising fear,
No premonition of a tear.

How, with a mirror, can you keep
Watch on your eyelids closed in sleep?
How judge which profile to bestow
On a new coin or cameo?
How, from two steps behind you, stare
At your firm nape discovered bare
Of ringlets as you bend and reach
Transparent pebbles from the beach?
Love, if you long for a surprise
Of self-discernment, hold my eyes
And plunge deep down in them to see
Sights never long withheld from me.

A Bracelet

A bracelet invisible
For your busy wrist,
Twisted from silver
Spilt afar,
From silver of the clear Moon,
From her sheer halo,
From the male beauty
Of a shooting star.

Hooded Flame

Love, though I sorrow, I shall never grieve:
Grief is to mourn a flame extinguished;
Sorrow, to find it hooded for the hour
When planetary influences deceive
And hope, like wine, turns sour.

The Crane

The Crane lounes loudly in his need,
    And so for love I loune:
Son to the sovereign Sun indeed,
    Courier of the Moon.

Her Brief Withdrawal

'Forgive me, love, if I withdraw awhile:
It is only that you ask such bitter questions,
Always another beyond the extreme last.
And the answers astound: you have entangled me
In my own mystery. Grant me a respite:
I was happier far, not asking, nor much caring,
Choosing by appetite only: self-deposed,
Self-reinstated, no one observing.
When I belittled this vibrancy of touch
And the active vengeance of these folded arms
No one could certify my powers for me
Or my saining virtue, or know that I compressed
Knots of destiny in a careless fist,
I who had passed for a foundling from the hills
Of innocent and flower-like fantasies,
Though minting silver by my mere tread . . . .
Did I not dote on you, I well might strike you
For implicating me in your true dream.'

Strangeness

You love me strangely, and in strangeness
I love you wholly, with no parallel
To this long miracle; for each example
Of love coincidence levels a finger
At strangeness undesigned as unforeseen.

And this long miracle is to discover
The inmost you and never leave her;
To show no curiosity for another;

To forge the soul and its desire together
Gently, openly and for ever.

Seated in silence, clothed in silence
And face to face – the room is small
But thronged with visitants –
We ask for nothing: we have all.

Song: *Though Once True Lovers*

Though once true lovers,
    We are less than friends.
What woman ever
    So ill-used her man?
That I played false
    Not even she pretends:
May God forgive her,
    For, alas, I can.

Song: *The Palm Tree*

Palm-tree, single and apart
    In your serpent-haunted land,
Like the fountain of a heart
    Soaring into air from sand –
None can count it as a fault
That your roots are fed with salt.

Panniers-full of dates you yield,
    Thorny branches laced with lights,
Wistful for no pasture-field
    Fed by torrents from a height,

Short of politics to share
With the damson or the pear.

Never-failing phoenix tree
   In your serpent-haunted land,
Fount of magic soaring free
   From a desert of salt sand;
Tears of joy are salty too –
Mine shall flow in praise of you.

Song: Dew-Drop and Diamond

The difference between you and her
(Whom I to you did once prefer)
Is clear enough to settle:
She like a diamond shone, but you
Shine like an early drop of dew
Poised on a red rose-petal.

The dew-drop carries in its eye
Mountain and forest, sea and sky,
With every change of weather;
Contrariwise, a diamond splits
The prospect into idle bits
That none can piece together.

Song: Just Friends

Just friend, you are my only friend –
You think the same of me
And swear our love must never end

Though lapped in secrecy,
As all true love should be.
They ask us: 'What about you two?'
I answer 'Only friends' and you:
'Just friends' gently agree.

Song: Sullen Moods

Love, never count your labour lost
  Though I turn sullen or retired
Even at your side; my thought is crossed
  With fancies by no evil fired.

And when I answer you, some days,
  Vaguely and wildly, never fear
That my love walks forbidden ways,
  Snapping the ties that hold it here.

If I speak gruffly, this mood is
  Mere indignation at my own
Shortcomings, plagues, uncertainties:
  I forget the gentler tone.

You, now that you have come to be
  My one beginning, prime and end,
I count at last as wholly me,
  Lover no longer nor yet friend.

Help me to see you as before
  When overwhelmed and dead, almost,
I stumbled on that secret door
  Which saves the live man from the ghost.

Be once again the distant light,
  Promise of glory, not yet known
In full perfection – wasted quite
  When on my imperfection thrown.

Possibly

Possibly is not a monosyllable;
  Then answer me
At once if possible
  Monosyllabically,
No will be good, *Yes* even better
Though longer by one letter.

Possibly is not a monosyllable,
  And my heart flies shut
At the warning rumble
  Of a suspended *But* . . .
O love, be brief and exact
In confession of simple fact.

Is Now the Time?

If he asks, 'Is now the time?', it is not the time.
She turns her head from his concern with time
  As a signal not to haste it;
And every time he asks: 'Is now the time?'
  A hundred nights are wasted.

Twins

Siamese twins: one, maddened by
The other's moral bigotry,
Resolved at length to misbehave
And drink them both into the grave.

Sail and Oar

Woman sails, man must row:
Each, disdainful of a tow,
Cuts across the other's bows
Shame or fury to arouse –
And evermore it shall be so,
Lest man sail, or woman row.

Gooseflesh Abbey

Nuns are allowed fully liberty of conscience.
Yet might this young witch, when she took the veil,
Count on an aged Abbess's connivance
At keeping toad-familiars in her cell?
Some called it liberty; but others, licence –
And how was she to tell?

Wigs and Beards

In the bad old days a bewigged country Squire
Would never pay his debts, unless at cards,
Shot, angled, urged his pack through standing grain,
Horsewhipped his tenantry, snorted at the arts,

Toped himself under the table every night,
Blasphemed God with a cropful of God-damns,
Aired whorehouse French or lame Italian,
Set fashions of pluperfect slovenliness
And claimed seigneurial rights over all women
Who slept, imprudently, under the same roof.

Taxes and wars long ago ploughed them under –
'And serve the bastards right' the Beards agree,
Hurling their empties through the café window
And belching loud as they proceed downstairs.
Latter-day bastards of that famous stock,
They never rode a nag, nor gaffed a trout,
Nor winged a pheasant, nor went soldiering,
But remain true to the same hell-fire code
In all available particulars
And scorn to pay their debts even at cards.
Moreunder (which is to subtract, not add),
Their ancestors called themselves gentlemen
As they, in the same sense, call themselves artists.

Astymelusa*

'Astymelusa!'
                    Knees at your approach
Suddenly give, more than in sleep or death –
As well they may; such love compels them.
'Astymelusa!'
                    But no answer comes.
Crowned with a leafy crown, the girl passes
Like a star afloat through glittering sky,
Or a golden flower, or drifted thistledown.

* A fragment by the Dorian Greek poet Alcman, seventh
century B.C., found among the Oxyrhynchus papyri.

To Be in Love

To spring impetuously in air and remain
Treading on air for three heart-beats or four,
Then to descend at leisure; or else to scale
The forward-tilted crag with no hand-holds;
Or, disembodied, to carry roses home
From a Queen's garden – this is being in love,
Graced with *agilitas* and *subtilitas*
At which few famous lovers ever guessed
Though children may foreknow it, deep in dream,
And ghosts may mourn it, haunting their own tombs,
And peacocks cry it, in default of speech.

Fact of the Act

On the other side of the world's narrow lane
You lie in bed, your young breasts tingling
With imagined kisses, your lips puckered,
Your fists tight.

Dreaming yourself naked in my arms,
Free from discovery, under some holm oak;
The high sun peering through thick branches,
All winds mute.

Endlessly you prolong the moment
Of your delirium: a first engagement,
Silent, inevitable, fearful,
Honey-sweet.

Will it be so in fact? Will fact mirror
Your virginal ecstasies:
True love, uncircumstantial,
No blame, no shame?

It is for you, now, to say 'come';
It is for you, now, to prepare the bed;
It is for you as the sole hostess
Of your white dreams –

It is for you to open the locked gate,
It is for you to shake red apples down,
It is for you to halve them with your hands
That both may eat.

Yet expectation lies as far from fact
As fact's own after-glow in memory;
Fact is a dark return to man's beginnings,
Test of our hardihood, test of a wilful
And blind acceptance of each other
As also flesh.

Within Reason

You have wandered widely through your own mind
And your own perfect body;
Thus learning, within reason, gentle one,
Everything that can prove worth the knowing.

A concise wisdom never attained by those
Bodiless nobodies
Who travel pen in hand through other's minds,
But without reason,
Feeding on manifold contradiction.

To stand perplexed by love's inconsequences
Like fire-flies in your hair
Or distant flashes of a summer storm:
Such are the stabs of joy you deal me
Who also wander widely through my mind
And still imperfect body.

She to Him

To have it, sweetheart, is to know you have it
Rather than think you have it;
To think you have it is a wish to take it,
Though afterwards you would not have it –
And thus a fear to take it.
Yet if you know you have it, you may take it
And know that still you have it.

The Yet Unsayable

It was always fiercer, brighter, gentler than could be told
Even in words quickened by Truth's dark eye:
Its absence, whirlpool; its presence, deluge;
Its time, astonishment; its magnitude,
A murderous dagger-point.
                              So we surrender
Our voices to the dried and scurrying leaves
And choose our own long-predetermined path
From the unsaid to the yet unsayable
In silence of love and love's temerity.

The Olive-Yard

Now by a sudden shift of eye
The hitherto exemplary world
Takes on immediate wildness
And birds, trees, winds, the very letters
Of our childhood's alphabet, alter
Into rainbowed mysteries.

Flesh is no longer flesh, but power;
Numbers, no longer arithmetical,
Dance like lambs, fly like doves;
And silence falls at last, though silken branches
Gently heave in the near olive-yard
And vague cloud labours on.

Whose was the stroke of summer genius
Flung from a mountain fastness
Where the griffon-vulture soars
That let us read our shrouded future
As easily as a book of prayer
Spread open on the knee?

The Narrow Sea

With you for mast and sail and flag,
And anchor never known to drag,
Death's narrow but oppressive sea
Looks not unnavigable to me.

Index of First Lines

A bitter year it was. What woman ever   141
A bracelet invisible   168
A difficult achievement for true lovers   138
A last poem, and a very last, and yet another – 145
Alas for obstinate doubt: the dread   143
'Alice, dear, what ails you'   20
Allie, call the birds in   21
All saints revile her, and all sober men   115
And glad to find, on again looking at it   62
Any honest housewife could sort them out   66
A perverse habit of cat-goddesses –   127
Are they blind, the lords of Gaza   28
A round moon suffocates the neighbouring stars   154
A simple nosegay! was that much to ask?   23
As I walked out that sultry night   46
'Astymelusa!'   175
A sunbeam on the well-waxed oak   87
At sunset, only to his true love   147
At the end of Tarriers' Lane, which was the street 60
At Viscount Nelson's lavish funeral   108

Bats at play taunt us with 'guess how many'   148
Bears gash the forest trees   106
Be assured, the Dragon is not dead   47
Beauty in trouble flees to the good angel   113
Below the ridge a raven flew   40
Beware, madam, of the witty devil   143
But if that Cerberus, my mind, should be   162
'But that was nothing to what things came out'   61
By moonlight   109
By sloth on sorrow fathered   95
By this exchange of eyes, this encirclement   152

Call it a good marriage –   133
Children are dumb to say how hot the day is   36
Children, if you dare to think   34
Close bound in a familiar bed   124
Come closer yet, my honeysuckle, my sweetheart Jinny   42
'Come, surly fellow, come: a song!'   15
Courtesies of good-morning and good-evening   69

Dear love, since the impossible proves   150
Desire, first, by a natural miracle   156
Downstairs a clock had chimed, two o'clock only   30
Down, wanton, down! Have you no shame   65
'Do you delude yourself?' a neighbour asks   137
Drowsing in my chair of disbelief   136
Dust in a cloud, blinding weather   29
Dying sun, shine warm a little longer!   119

Every choice is always the wrong choice   150

Far away is close at hand   40
Finis, apparent on an earlier page   153
Five summer days, five summer nights   128
Forewarned of madness   82
For fear strangers might intrude upon us   158
'Forgive me, love, if I withdraw awhile   169
For me, the naked and the nude   131
Fugitive firs and larches for a moment   86

Goths, Vandals, Huns, Isaurian mountaineers   76
Grey haunted eyes, absent-mindedly glaring   135
Grieve for the loveless, spiritless, faceless men   154
Guns from the sea open against us   94

Have you not read   98
Heather and holly   166
He had done for her all that a man could   146
He is quick, thinking in clear images   57

181

High on his figured couch beyond the waves   5
His appearances are incalcuable   13
His eyes are quickened so with grief   2
How most unnatural-seeming, yet how proper   11
How often have I said before   15
Husks, rags and bones, waste-paper, excrement   6

I'd die for you or you for me   14
If he asks, 'Is now the time?', it is not the time   17
If strange things happen where she is   7
In a deep thought of you and concentration   8
In Northern seas there roams a fish called K'un   16
Interalienation of their hearts   16
In the bad old days a bewigged country Squire   17
In time all undertakings are made good   14
Into a gentle wilderness and confusion   5
Into exile with only a few shirts   7
It is a poet's privilege and fate   12
It was always fiercer, brighter, gentler than could be told 17

Just friend, you are my only friend   17

Lady, lovely lady   2
Lest men suspect your tale to be untrue   5
Let me tell you the story of how I began   5
Like a lizard in the sun, though not scuttling   7
Living among orchards, we are ruled   10
Look forward, truant, to your second childhood   10
Looking by chance in at the open window   8
Lost manor where I walk continually   2
Louder than gulls the little children scream   10
'Love at first sight,' some say, misnaming   6
Love is a universal migraine   13
Lovliest flowers, though crooked in their border   5
Love, never count your labour lost   172
Lovers in the act dispense   9

Love, though I sorrow, I shall never grieve   168
Love without hope, as when the young bird-catcher   23

My Chinese uncle, gouty, deaf, half-blinded   110
My heart lies wrapped in red under your pillow   155
My New Year's drink is mulled to-night   38

Never be disenchanted of   103
Never forget who brings the rain   138
Never was so profound a shadow thrown   158
No argument, no anger, no remorse   144
Nobody, ancient mischief, nobody   45
Not of father nor of mother   116
Not to sleep all the night long, for pure joy   149
Now by a sudden shift of eye   179
Nuns are allowed fully liberty of conscience   174

Often, half-way to sleep   32
On a clear day how thin the horizon   140
On her shut lids the lightning flickers   130
On the other side of the world's narrow lane   176
O the clear moment, when from the mouth   57
Out shines again the glorious round sun   159
O what astonishment if you   167
Owls – they whinny down the night   18

Pale at first and cold   16
Palm-tree, single and apart   170
Pass now in metaphor beyond birds   157
Peace, the wild valley streaked with torrents   124
Possibly is not a monosyllable   173
Presage and caveat not only seem   128

Rising early and walking in the garden   58

Seldom yet now: the quality   139
She is no liar, yet she will wash away   145

She listened to his voice urgently pleading   155
She speaks always in her own voice   123
She tells her love while half asleep   103
She, then, like snow in a dark night   77
Should the building totter, run for an archway!   90
Siamese twins: one, maddened by   174
Since now in every public place   127
Small gnats that fly   20
Some of you may know, others perhaps can guess   134
So, overmasterful, to sea!   51
So soon as ever your mazed spirit descends   117
Stirring suddenly from long hibernation   100
Sulkily the sticks burn, and though they crackle   102

That aged woman with the bass voice   90
The bards falter in shame, their running verse   38
The blind are their own brothers; we   159
The Bower-bird improvised a cool retreat   161
The butterfly, a cabbage-white   56
The Crane lounes loudly in his need   168
The difference between you and her   171
The curious heart plays with its fears   94
The far side of your moon is black   152
The first heaven is a flowery plain   148
The full moon easterly rising, furious   93
The impartial Law enrolled a name   106
The King of Hearts a broadsword bears   147
The mind's eye sees as the heart mirrors   97
The parson to his pallid spouse   120
The patriarchal bed with four posts   92
The Rector's pallid neighbour at The Firs   101
There is one story and one story only   104
There was this road   54
These acres, always again lost   63
The seven years' curse is ended now   44
The suicide, far from content   98
'The sum of all the parts of Such —'   65

The vague sea thuds against the marble cliffs 67
This ancient house so notable 83
This honest wife, challenged at dusk 81
This is a wild land, country of my choice 17
This they know well: the Goddess yet abides 142
These famous men of old, the Ogres – 70
Those who dare give nothing 160
Though cruel seas like mountains fill the bay 140
Though once true lovers 170
Three blank walls, a barred window with no view 68
To beguile and betray, though pardonable in women 146
To be homeless is a pride 78
To bring the dead to life 74
To die with a forlorn hope, but soon to be raised 112
To evoke posterity 75
To find a garden-tulip growing 88
To go in no direction 42
To have it, sweetheart, is to know you have it 178
To spring inpetuously in air and remain 176
To the galleys, thief, and sweat your soul out 31
To the much-tossed Ulysses, never done 52
To walk on hills is to employ legs 72
Trapped in a dismal marsh, he told his troops 155
Truth-loving Persians do not dwell upon 108
Twined together and, as is customary 71

Unicorn with burning heart 162

Variegated flowers, nuts, cockle-shells 165

Walking with a virgin heart 24
Walls, mounds, enclosing corrugations 43
We have reached the end of pastime, for always 89
We looked, we loved, and therewith instantly 48
We stood together, side by side, rooted 151
We were not ever of their feline race 99
What did I dream? I do not know – 23

What happens afterwards, none need enquire 4
What, keep love in *perspective*? – that old lie 166
When all is over and you march for home 129
When first we came together 16
When I reached his place 49
When mountain rocks and leafy trees 60
When she came suddenly in 102
When that prime heroine of our nation, Alice 30
When the immense drugged universe explodes 157
Whether it was your way of walking 115
Who on your breast pillows his head now 120
Why have such scores of lovely, gifted girls 134
Why say 'death'? Death is neither harsh nor kind 41
With you for mast and sail and flag 179
Woman sails, man must row 174

You chose a lion to be your lover – 142
You have wandered widely through your own mind 172
You'll not forget these rocks and what I told you? 123
You, love, and I 119
You love me strangely, and in strangeness 169
You reading over my shoulder, peering beneath 53
You reject the rainbow 164
Your grieving moonlight face looks down 10
You weep whole heartedly – your shining tears 150

MORE ABOUT PENGUINS

Penguinews, which appears every month, contains details of all the new books issued by Penguins as they are published. From time to time it is supplemented by *Penguins in Print*, which is a complete list of all available books published by Penguins. (There are well over three thousand of these.)

A specimen copy of *Penguinews* will be sent to you free on request, and you can become a subscriber for the price of the postage. For a year's issues (including the complete lists) please send 30p if you live in the United Kingdom, or 60p if you live elsewhere. Just write to Dept EP, Penguin Books Ltd, Harmondsworth, Middlesex, enclosing a cheque or postal order, and your name will be added to the mailing list.

Note: *Penguinews* and *Penguins in Print* are not available in the U.S.A. or Canada

Penguin Modern European Poets

Selected Poems
Apollinaire

Guillaume Apollinaire was a friend and supporter of the Cubists. His own experimental poetic forms employ rhythms which dispense with punctuation and a style of typography derived from exercises on postcards sent from the front in the First World War. Yet he is also in France the last of the poets whose lines young people know by heart.

'He said that poetry is a power to transform even the dullest activities of the mind, to waken the consciousness to a more vivid awareness, and to make everything more exciting and more fascinating. This is what he himself did.' – *Sir Maurice Bowra*

Rimbaud: Selected Verse

Paul Claudel called Rimbaud 'a mystic in the savage state'. All his poetry was written between the ages of sixteen and nineteen, after which he showed no interest in literature or in his literary reputation but became a trader in Abyssinia, A symbolist, much influenced by Baudelaire for his themes and by Verlaine for his harmonic effects, Rimbaud was yet a most individual poet. He was determined to 'reach the un-known' through his poetry and believed that the poet should undergo the 'complete dislocation of all the senses', in order to enlarge experience and to achieve self-know-ledge.

This dislocation of the senses is shown most clearly in *Les Illuminations* and may have been obtained by taking hashish or opium. It is a mystery why this poet, who ex-celled in the creation of startling images, and wrote some of the most original and moving works of French literature, gave up writing so young. In his introduction to this Penguin selection Oliver Bernard suggests that this may have been because he had hoped through alchemy and poetry to be-come 'god-like' and turned away in disgust when he found he had failed.

This edition, which includes some 140 poems, contains an introduction and plain prose translations by Oliver Bernard, himself a poet and the author of *Country Matters and Other Poems*.

Poem into Poem
World Poetry in Modern Verse Translation
Edited by George Steiner

Poem into Poem is the only book of its kind. In an anthology
of verse translations from twenty-two languages (ranging
from ancient Hebrew and Greek to modern Chinese), each
one has been made by an English or American poet who not
only renders the original but also creates what is a living
poem in its own right.

We find extraordinary encounters – Hardy and Sappho,
Hopkins and Horace, Yeats and Ronsard, Scott Fitzgerald
and Rimbaud, James Joyce and Gottfried Keller, Ezra Pound
and Sophocles. The light of another poem is caught in a live
mirror.

George Steiner believes that translation is central to the
nature of modern poetry; that ours is the most brilliant
period of poetic translation and recapture since the Eliza-
bethans. This anthology contains his evidence.

Not for sale in the U.S.A. or Canada

Works by Robert Graves
available in Penguins and Pelicans

I, Claudius

Robert Graves' magnificent reconstruction of the grandeur and folly and vileness of Imperial Rome.

Claudius the God

In the sequel to *I, Claudius* a republican Roman Emperor writes the inside story of his reign.

In one of the finest historical reconstructions of the century Robert Graves has created a character to compare with Dostoyevsky's Prince Myshkin.

Goodbye To All That

Robert Graves' autobiography first appeared in 1929.

'It is a permanently valuable work of literary art, and indispensable for the historian either of the First World War or of modern English poetry ... This book has also the interest of being one of the most candid self-portraits of a poet, warts and all, ever painted. The sketches of friends of Mr Graves, like T. E. Lawrence, are beautifully vivid.' – *The Times Literary Supplement*

also available

COLLECTED SHORT STORIES

ANTIGUA, PENNY, PUCE

WIFE TO MR MILTON

THE GREEK MYTHS (in two volumes) Pelican*

COUNT BELISARIUS

and in collaboration with Alan Hodge

THE LONG WEEKEND
(A Social History of Great Britain 1918-1939)

Robert Graves has also written a fine translation of *The Golden Ass* by Apuleius, and of *The Twelve Caesars* by Suetonius, for the Penguin Classic series.

*Available in the U.S.A.